Plottr

Plan Your Books Like a Pro

The Future of Book Outlining is Already Here

www.plottr.com/future

Leader SOURCEFORGE Spring 2023

Capterra 4.9 ★★★★★

Software Suggest Trending WINTER 2023

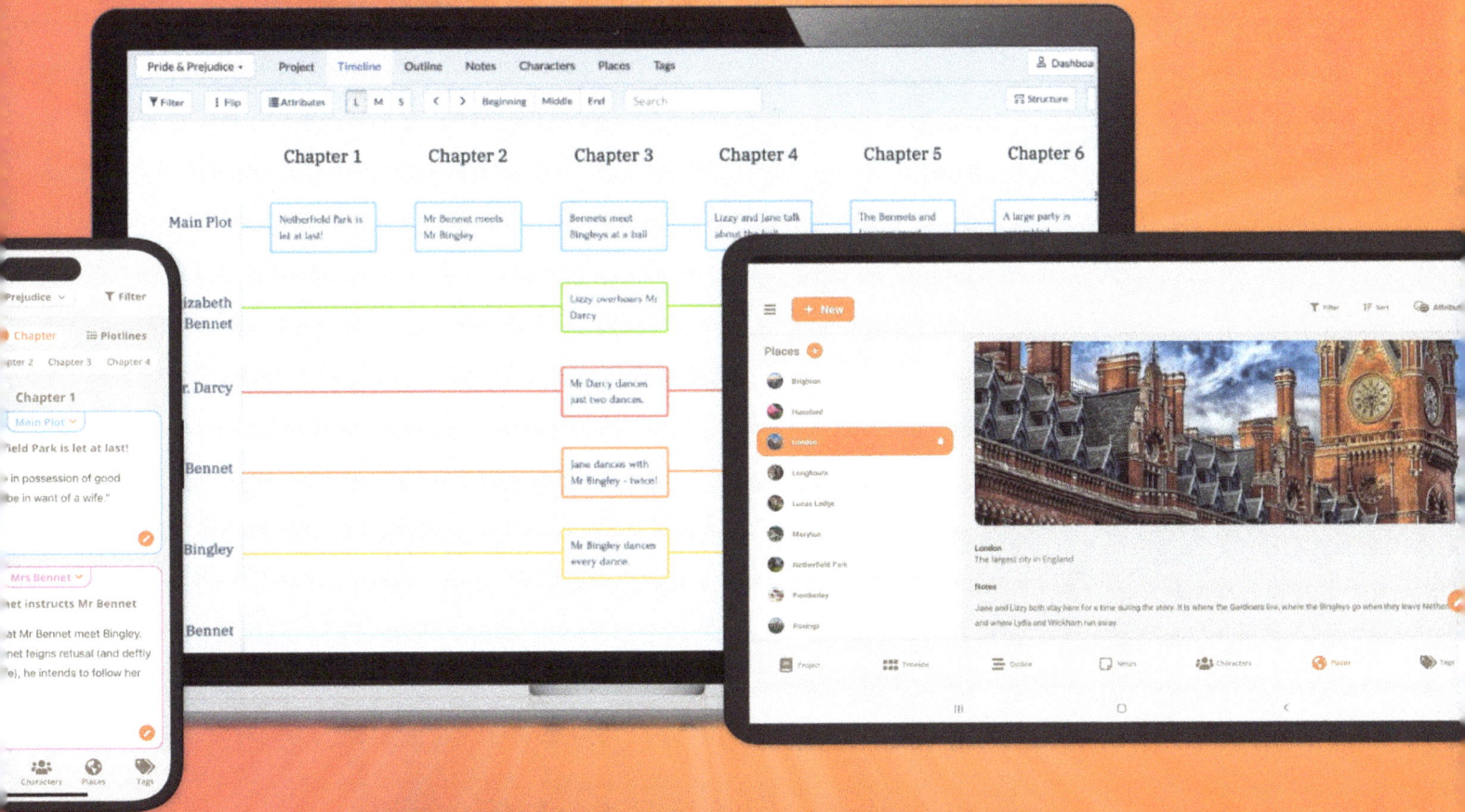

![Alliance of Independent Authors logo] **Alliance of Independent Authors**

FOR SELF-PUBLISHING **NOVELISTS, POETS** AND **NON-FICTION AUTHORS**

Unlock your full potential as an Independent Author

Access the support and resources of the Alliance of Independent Authors

Join the world's only non-profit professional writing organization representing independent authors globally.

Harness a wealth of resources, expertise, and community support, all tailored for you and your books.

- Tools & Resources
- Mentors & Advisors
- Legal & Rights
- Member Support Desk
- Webinars & Workshops
- Vibrant Community
- Discounts & Deals
- Free guidebooks, handbooks and member magazine

Creative Self-Publishing
ALLi's Guide to Independent Publishing for Authors and Poets
Orna A. Ross

Choose the Best Self-Publishing Services
ALLi's Guide to Assembling Your Tools and Your Team
John Doppler

Reach More Readers, Sell More Books
ALLi's Guide to Book Marketing for Authors and Poets
Orna A. Ross

Your Book in Bookstores
ALLi's Guide to Print Book Distribution for Authors
Debbie P. Young

150 Self-Publishing Questions Answered
ALLi's Writing, Publishing, & Book Marketing Tips for Authors and Poets
M.L. Ronn

How Authors License Publishing Rights
ALLi's Guide to Working with Publishers, Producers and Others
Orna A. Ross

Become a member today, visit:
www.allianceindependentauthors.org/join
or Scan the QR code

> "I joined while having a crisis with Amazon KDP... The Alliance is a beacon of light. I recommend that all indie authors join..."
> **Susan Marshall**

> "The Alliance is about standing together."
> **Joanna Penn**

> "It's the good stuff, all on one place."
> **Richard Wright**

> "ALLi has helped me in myriad ways: discounts on services, vetting providers, charting a course to sales success. But more than anything it's a community of friendly, knowledgeable, helpful people."
> **Beth Duke**

See hundreds more testimonials at:
AllianceIndependentAuthors.org/testimonials

IAM
ALL ABOUT THE MONEY

PLANNING TRAVEL TO A CONFERENCE?

Use miles.

Explore ways to make the most of your award miles.

Writelink.to/unitedair

Authorpreneurs in Action

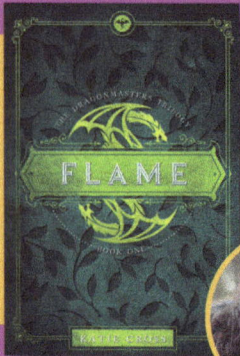

"I love Lulu! They've been a fantastic distributor of my paperbacks and an excellent partner as I dive into direct sales. They integrate so smoothly with my personal Shopify store, and their customer support has been top notch."

Katie Cross, katiecrossbooks.com

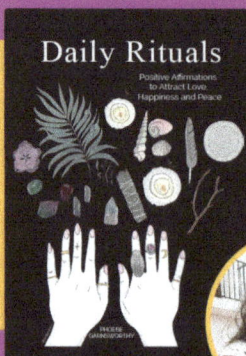

"Having my own store has given me the freedom to look at my creativity as a profitable business and lifelong career."

Phoebe Garnsworthy, phoebegarnsworthy.com

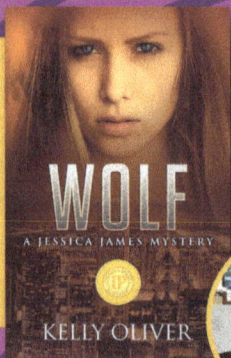

"Lulu has a super handy integration with Shopify. Lulu makes it so easy to sell paperbacks directly to readers."

Kelly Oliver, kellyoliverbooks.com

"My experience with Lulu Direct has been more convenient and simple than I anticipated or thought possible. I simply publish, take a step back and allow the well-oiled machine to run itself. Most grateful!"

Molly McGivern, theactorsalmanac.com

lulu*direct*

Sell Smarter, Not Harder.

Sell Books from Your Website Using Lulu Direct

Keep 100% of your profit

Retain customer data

Integrate with Shopify, WooCommerce, Zapier, & Custom API

Get paid quickly

No monthly fees

Fully automated white-label fulfillment

Global print network

B Corp Certified

Dropshipping Multiple Orders for a New Book Launch or Crowdfunding Campaign? Use the Lulu Order Import Tool!

We make dropshipping multiple orders at once easier than ever!

- ☑ Upload your book on Lulu for free
- ☑ Use the Order Import Tool to upload a file with your customer's order and shipping information
- ☑ We'll professionally print the orders and drop ship each one to your fans around the world

Get exclusive Publishing & Marketing tips to help you create and sell your books more effectively!

INDIE
AUTHOR MAGAZINE

EDITORIAL

Publisher | Chelle Honiker

Editor in Chief | Nicole Schroeder

Creative Director | Alice Briggs

Partner Relationship Manager | Elaine Bateman

ADVERTISING & MARKETING

Inquiries
Ads@AtheniaCreative.com

Information
Partner.IndieAuthorMagazine.com

CONTRIBUTORS

Angela Archer, Elaine Bateman, Bradley Charbonneau, Jackie Dana, Heather Clement Davis, Jamie Davis, Laurel Decher, Gill Fernley, Jen B. Green, Marion Hermannsen, Jenn Lessmann, Megan Linski-Fox, Angie Martin, Merri Maywether, Kevin McLaughlin, Jenn Mitchell, Tanya Nellestein, Susan Odev, Eryka Parker, Tiffany Robinson, Robyn Sarty, Joe Solari, David Viergutz

SUBSCRIPTIONS
https://indieauthormagazine.com/subscribe/

HOW TO READ
https://indieauthormagazine.com/how-to-read/

WHEN WRITING MEANS BUSINESS
IndieAuthorMagazine.com

Athenia Creative | 6820 Apus Dr., Sparks, NV, 89436 USA | 775.298.1925
ISSN 2768-7880 (online)–ISSN 2768-7872 (print)

The publication, authors, and contributors reserve their rights in regards to copyright of their work. No part of this work covered by the copyright may be reproduced or copied in any form or by any means without the written consent of the publisher. All copyrighted work was reproduced with the permission of the owner.

Reasonable care is taken to ensure that *Indie Author Magazine* articles and other information on the website are up to date and as accurate as possible, at the time of publication, but no responsibility can be taken by *Indie Author Magazine* for any errors or omissions contained herein. Furthermore, *Indie Author Magazine* takes no responsibility for any losses, damages, or distress resulting from adherence to any information made available through this publication. The opinions expressed are those of the authors and do not necessarily reflect the views of *Indie Author Magazine*.

THE NEW WAY FOR READERS TO FIND AUTHORS SELLING DIRECT

DIRECT2READERS

A unique directory where you can connect directly with your fans and keep all your hard-earned profits.

💡 Innovative Recommendation Engine: Our natural language recommendation engine helps readers discover books based on their preferences. Say goodbye to clunky categories!

📈 New Market Access: Gain exposure to a new segment of avid readers, all hungry for fresh indie voices.

💵 Zero Commissions: You read it right! We don't take a cut. Your profits are yours to keep.

🚀 Boost Your Sales: Benefit from our advanced marketing and influencer channels designed to supercharge your direct sales.

🌐 **Register Now**
Direct2Readers.com

From the
EDITOR IN CHIEF

Blame it on how invested I am in superhero movies, but I am paranoid about spoilers. If I'm worried about encountering a leaked plot twist from a movie, book, or game, I will take a social media hiatus and resort to childhood playground levels of avoidance: plugging my ears and shouting "la, la, la" until the danger has passed.

But I make an exception for Horror. I cannot handle the genre—and the only way I can is by immediately reading the complete synopsis, spoilers and all, so there are no surprises lurking around the corner.

I've never been a fan of Horror. In my previous magazine job before joining *IAM*, I even wrote an article in which I tried to discover the secret to enjoying it. But the terrifying truth about Horror, at least for scaredy-cats like me, is that it isn't going anywhere. From 1700s Gothic literature to modern-day slasher films turned blockbuster hits, people have always craved the genre. It taps into our instinctual desire to survive and makes us feel that we've truly lived through the perils of the story alongside the main character.

As much as I may try, it's also unavoidable. Horror promises its audience a certain level of spine-tingling spookiness, but as both *Trope Thesaurus* author Jennifer Hilt and *IAM* staff writer and Horror author David Viergutz point out in this month's issue, its standout tropes can also show up in any genre. The "final girl" trope is just as relevant in Fairy-Tale Retellings, and "the impostor hidden in plain sight" is a favorite among Mystery authors. Romance readers love the "forbidden fruit" trope as much as Horror readers—even if there is a happier ending for one set of characters than another.

Horror as a genre may have me hiding my face in my hands, but horror as an emotion is essential to good storytelling. And like any good Horror villain, it's always there, hiding in the shadows and biding its time, no matter the stories you write …

Use it cautiously, authors.

Nicole Schroeder
Editor in Chief
Indie Author Magazine

Nicole Schroeder is a storyteller at heart. As the editor in chief of Indie Author Magazine, she brings nearly a decade of journalism and editorial experience to the publication, delighting in any opportunity to tell true stories and help others do the same. She holds a bachelor's degree from the Missouri School of Journalism and minors in English and Spanish. Her previous work includes editorial roles at local publications, and she's helped edit and produce numerous fiction and nonfiction books, including a Holocaust survivor's memoir, alongside independent publishers. Her own creative writing has been published in national literary magazines. When she's not at her writing desk, Nicole is usually in the saddle, cuddling her guinea pigs, or spending time with family. She loves any excuse to talk about Marvel movies and considers National Novel Writing Month its own holiday.

929 PRESS

Empowering Storytellers in a Digital Landscape

WE HELP STORYTELLERS BLEND THEIR ART WITH INNOVATIVE DIGITAL TOOLS TO CAPTIVATE AUDIENCES ACROSS ALL PLATFORMS

➤ EBook, Print & Audiobook Design & Formatting

➤ iOS and Google Play Apps

➤ Digital & Print Magazine Design & Distribution

➤ Website Design & Social Media Branding

929PRESS.COM

What's Your Mindset around Money?

There is a common belief that artists, including authors, make very little money. To explore that assumption, in 2023, the Alliance of Independent Authors (ALLi) commissioned the world's first Indie Author Income Survey, focused specifically on self-published authors. We found that indie authors earn more than those who are traditionally published, and this data was confirmed later that year by a survey conducted by the Authors Guild of traditionally and indie-published authors.

In addition to the author survey, which ALLi will repeat every two years, ALLi also compiles the Big Indie Author Data Drop, which brings together facts and figures from across the self-publishing industry. This type of information is a vital resource for authors making strategic and tactical decisions about their publishing business. All these reports are available at https://www.allianceindependentauthors.org/facts.

Regardless of how developed or extensive your publishing business is, following these two guidelines is critical:

When you decide to self-publish, you become a publisher, and publishing is a business. A business owner invests money to make more money, so you'll

do best if you think less about how much something costs and think instead about how much return you can expect from that investment.

Value your time as much as your money. Although you can often avoid making a financial investment by investing time instead, both have value; one might argue that your time is your most valuable commodity. Paying for assistance or a tool might yield better financial results than trying to do everything yourself.

The indie authors who are succeeding financially are those who are treating their writing and publishing work as the business it is, and who bring a healthy money mindset to their work. In this article, we share tips for the steps authors can take at every level to optimize their business for financial success.

BEGINNING AUTHORS: ESTABLISH THE BASICS AND INVEST WISELY

ALLi aims to empower every writer who commits to high-quality indie publishing. We know that meeting professional publishing standards can be a financial challenge for some authors, especially those just starting out. A genre-right cover design and a professional edit can represent an investment of $1,000 or more. But modest financial resources shouldn't put the goal of high-quality work out of reach. If you don't have money to invest, ALLi provides guidance on how to get started with little or no expenditure in our guide *Self-Publishing (Almost) for Free*, which you can download here: https://www.allianceindependentauthors.org/campaigns/selfpub3.

In addition, here are a few pointers for beginning authors who are getting their publishing business up and running:

Log all your writing business money coming in and out—even a basic spreadsheet will do—so that you can monitor your finances on an ongoing basis and review past performance to look for opportunities to optimize in the future.

Set aside money to pay your taxes throughout the year.

When considering where to invest your educational time and money, factor in business classes as well as craft classes.

ALLi's three-part series on money management for indie authors covers the basic money principles and mindset that authors should develop. Find the series on ALLi's blog:

- https://selfpublishingadvice.org/embracing-a-positive-money-mindset
- https://selfpublishingadvice.org/money-basics-for-indie-authors-part-two-the-top-financial-terms-indie-authors-need-to-know
- https://selfpublishingadvice.org/money-management-principles-for-indie-authors-self-publishing-money-basics-part-three

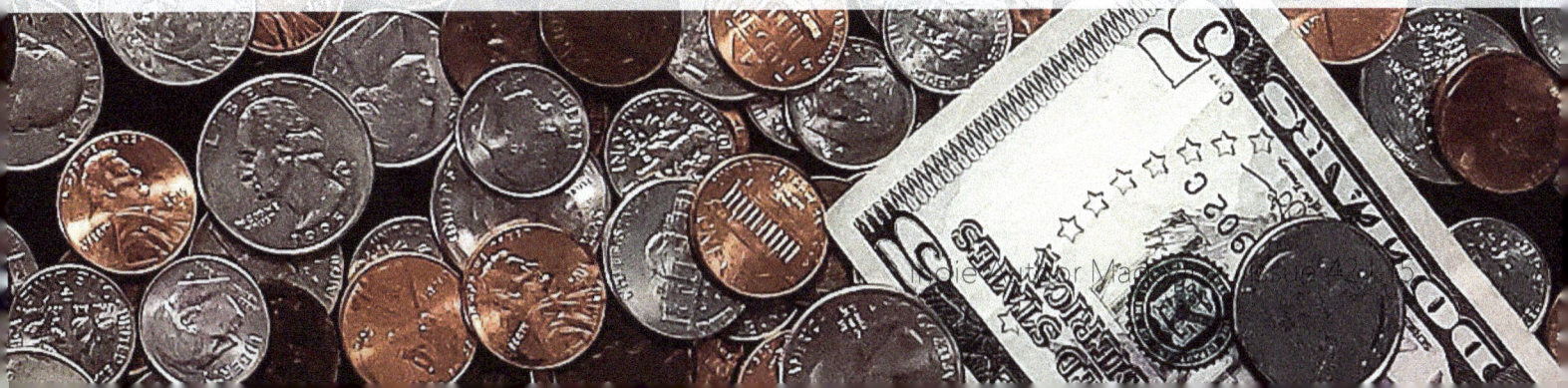

FOR EMERGING AUTHORS: KEEP UPGRADING YOUR MONEY MINDSET

As you develop your author business, continue to work on your money mindset: how you think and behave around money. Often people have ways of behaving that are detrimental to their financial success.

If you believe it's wrong to make money from helping people, then you might be tempted to give away your self-help book with no solid business reason for doing so.

If you somehow feel that indie authors are less worthy than traditionally published authors, you may price your books lower than theirs, even if the quality is the same.

If you have heard "artists are flaky" once too often, you might believe you will be no good with money and not bother to keep proper records rather than learning how to do so, just as you learned the craft of writing.

For more information on the importance of a money mindset and for tips to help you develop yours, check out ALLi's March 13, 2024, podcast episode and transcript, "Pen to Prosperity: Money Mindset, Manifestation, and Management with Carissa Andrews": https://selfpublishingadvice.org/podcast-money-mindset.

FOR EXPERIENCED AUTHORS: KEEP LEARNING

There's a reason ALLi's top tier of author membership—authors who sell over fifty thousand books a year—is called Authorpreneur: if you want to be a successful author in terms of sales, you will need to think like an entrepreneur. At this stage, with a little more budget available and probably a significant back catalog, think about expanding your money mindset with the following steps.

Make sure you're thinking of each piece of content as a core piece of creative IP whose value you can maximize through multiple formats and selective rights licensing.

Get a financial advisor and professional accountant, and make sure that they have experience working with authors and that they understand the publishing industry. Tapping into their expertise will pay back your investment.

Consider pursuing a relationship with a literary agent who can broker more complex deals for you and maximize your income through opportunities like translations and film deals.

Make provisions for financial benefits from your work for your beneficiaries. Creative works have a seventy-year "life" after the death of their creators, during which time they remain in copyright and can generate money for the creator's estate. However, only a quarter of authors have made any provision for their literary estate in their wills. ALLi members can take advantage of two guidebooks by Michael La Ronn to provide guidelines for managing your author estate: *The Author Estate Handbook: How to Organize Your Affairs and Leave a Legacy* and *The Author Heir Handbook: How to Manage an Author Estate and Look After a Legacy.*

FOR ALL AUTHORS

On ALLi's *Self-Publishing Advice & Inspirations* podcast, ALLi founder Orna Ross and advisor Joanna Penn shared how to optimize your earning potential in a March 2023 episode, "How to Make More Money than the Average Author." Listen at https://selfpublishingadvice.org/make-more-money.

As an indie author publisher, understanding money and having a positive mindset about it is critical to the success of your publishing business. Recognizing that you are an entrepreneur as well as a creator will lay the foundation for a successful author career. ∎

Matty Dalrymple, ALLi Campaigns Manager

Matty Dalrymple, ALLi Campaigns Manager

The Alliance of Independent Authors (ALLi) is a global membership association for self-publishing authors. A non-profit, our mission is ethics and excellence in self-publishing. Everyone on our team is a working indie author and we offer advice and advocacy for self-publishing authors within the literary, publishing and creative industries around the world. www.allianceindependentauthors.org

Dear Indie Annie,

I'm still in the "side hustle" stage of my career, and I sometimes struggle with deciding whether larger costs—platform subscriptions, conference tickets, a specific editor or cover designer, ads—are a good investment or something that should wait until I'm earning more from my books. Any tips?

Trying to Be a Smart Spender

Dear Trying to Be a Smart Spender,

Oh, darling Spender, managing your author finances is trickier than solving a Rubik's Cube blindfolded! But fear not, we'll untangle this colorful conundrum together.

Think of building your writing career as tending to a beloved garden. When nurturing any verdant plot, it is important to give most attention to the literal roots of your enterprise. You cannot do everything at once, so clear away the debris and concentrate on what will create the best environment for your plants to grow. For example, some investments are seeds that need planting now for future harvests, while others are akin to fancy garden gnomes that can wait until your plot is more established.

Now, personally, and this may shock my gentle readers, I am partial to a cheeky gnome or two scattered here and there, but they will not provide me with a bountiful harvest. And back-breaking though it may be, I know that to create a garden that will bring me pleasure and sustenance in the years to come, I have to spend time on the basics first.

Quality editing is one essential seed, for example, and eye-catching covers are your foundation plants—the roses and evergreens that give structure to your authorial landscape. Skimp here, and you might as well be planting plastic flowers! A meager yield indeed.

Platform subscriptions and ads are your fertilizer and plant food. Used judiciously, they nourish rapid growth. But overdoing it can burn your delicate seedlings. So start with small doses, testing which blend helps your particular species of stories thrive.

Got burning questions about the wibbly-wobbly world of indie authoring? Eager to unravel the mysteries of publishing, writing woes, or anything in between? Give your quizzical quills a whirl and shoot your musings over to indieannie@indieauthormagazine.com. Your inky quandaries are my cup of tea!

Conferences and networking events? They're the gardening club meetings of the author world, valuable for knowledge and connections. And, my darling Spender, it's fantastic to visit other gardens for inspiration and seed swapping, but not strictly necessary for your garden to thrive. Begin with local garden club meetings before jetting off to the Chelsea Flower Show of writing conferences.

Remember the tale of Jack and his magic beans? Sometimes a seemingly frivolous expense can lead to unexpected golden eggs. But unlike Jack, do your research before trading the family cow!

Look to savvy indie gardeners who've cultivated lush literary landscapes from humble beginnings. Andy Weir self-published *The Martian* with minimal upfront costs before it blossomed into a bestseller and Hollywood blockbuster. E.L. James started with fanfiction before the Fifty Shades series grew into an empire.

Remember, even the mightiest oaks start as tiny acorns. Look at Margaret Atwood, who began by self-publishing a poetry pamphlet before her garden grew into the lush forest of *The Handmaid's Tale* and beyond. Or consider Hugh Howey, who planted *Wool* as a short story before it grew into a self-published sensation.

My budding literary landscaper, invest wisely in your plot's foundation. Nurture those vital seeds with quality soil (editing) and attractive pots (covers). Use fertilizer (marketing) judiciously, and save the ornate topiary and koi ponds for when your garden's overflowing with literary fruits.

Remember, every flourishing author's garden started with a single well-tended seed. With patience, smart investments, and a green thumb for storytelling, your literary oasis will soon be the envy of the neighborhood!

Happy writing,
Indie Annie
X

10 TIPS FOR
SELLING WIDER THAN WIDE

Plenty of authors these days talk about new opportunities beyond the major retailers. As indie publishing expands into new territories and readers are searching out new ways of interacting with the stories they love, authors are moving to take advantage of how we can sell our books wider than wide, looking for places where we can find new readers to delight and entertain.

As authors look to expand their reach beyond more obvious book retailers, crowdfunding campaigns—usually Kickstarter—direct sales from an author's website, and reader subscriptions on sites such as Substack and Patreon have emerged as some of the most popular options. A full rundown of those sales channels is too big for any single article, but here are a few tips to help maximize your use of each of these possibilities.

CROWDFUNDING

1 BE PREPARED TO START SMALL.

One good way to think about crowdfunding sites is like they're a new retailer. They can be a good place to earn new fans and build readership. But like any new venue, it can take a while to build up an audience. It's not unusual to start small and gradually grow with each new project. Starting with a relatively small—but not so small as to be unprofitable—goal can be a powerful way to build your Kickstarter empire. Often something as simple as a $500 target can work well, assuming your budget works out.

2 USE E-BOOKS AS EXTRAS.

Only part of the revenue from a crowdfunding campaign comes from the actual project. One can also derive a lot of income from add-ons, and e-books are an easy and popular option—that doesn't cost you as the author anything additional to produce or distribute. If you have another series of books that have a similar target reader to the project you're trying to fund, use them as add-ons; many readers will pick up some or all of them.

③ PHYSICAL REWARDS ARE THE MAIN DRIVERS.

The best-funding crowdfunding campaigns usually have a physical product as the main reward, according to Anthea Sharp, author of *Kickstarter for Authors*, and Monica Leonelle, co-author of *Get Your Book Selling on Kickstarter*, so this is generally a good direction to travel, especially for your first attempts at crowdfunding. Running a crowdfunding event for something digital, like an audiobook, tends to be much more challenging as the platform market is smaller, so you may need to focus more on bringing an audience for these projects. Because of this, it's often best to begin with something easier, like a special edition hardcover of the book your fans already love most, or a print and e-book launch of a new book or trilogy.

SUBSCRIPTION PLATFORMS

---

④ CONSISTENCY MATTERS.

For writing in general, consistency can help a lot with maintaining creative momentum. But it's especially crucial when we ask readers to pay us monthly for content. Make sure the content you promise readers—and the deadlines you've set for writing it—is achievable regularly. If for some reason you can't deliver what you've promised, the best practice is to be transparent with supporters and communicate clearly what's going on.

Pro Tip: Authors often talk about batch-creating social media posts or newsletter content to save time, and you can do the same with subscription platforms. If you can set targets that are consistently reachable, so that you can over time build up some backlog of things to post, then you're in great shape to deliver what your readers expect even if you aren't able to hit your target every once in a while.

---

⑤ OFFER E-BOOKS AS SIGN-UP BONUSES.

There are a few ways to maximize the use of already published e-books with subscriptions, but one method is to offer them as bonuses to entice new subscribers, similar to how many use reader magnets to pull readers into their newsletter. Methods vary for how to do this, but the two most popular seem to be offering an EPUB as a bonus for download when someone subscribes or having a "subscriber library" of already completed books available for subscribers, usually right on the subscription site. E-books published in Kindle Unlimited (KU) won't be eligible, but for those published wide, these bonuses make readers feel like they're snagging a deal.

6 **FOLLOW THE TRAJECTORY: 'SUBSCRIPTION' TO 'FREE' TO 'PUBLISHED.'**
The workflow many subscription-using authors prefer is sharing new writing first with subscribers, then with online readers, and finally as a completed published work. They publish chapters to their paid subscribers as they write them. Later, they release those chapters for free on Wattpad, Royal Road, or similar sites, dripping them out at the same pace they're writing new ones. The subscription always stays ahead, sometimes forty chapters or more, of the free releases, with top tiers usually getting content three to five months ahead of the free release. This encourages fans to sign up to find out what happens next sooner. Later still, those chapters are compiled into books, edited, and published on retailers. For wide authors, the special advantage here is that non-KU books don't have to be taken down from the free sites or subscription site, allowing the subscription-generating engine to continue purring along.

DIRECT SALES

7 **IT'S OK TO START SELLING E-BOOKS ON YOUR WEBSITE.**
"Direct sales" may sound like it requires a leap into ordering, shipping, and managing the distribution of physical copies, but starting out with e-books is often easier. Since there's no need to get set up with a printer, it takes a major step out of the loop. This is one area where wide authors can especially shine, since they can immediately set up all their e-books for direct sales and go from making 70 percent of list price to about 90 percent to 95 percent per copy. Adding print is great too, of course, but it's OK to start with one product and then expand.

8 **DIRECT SALES OF PRINT BOOKS ARE POWERFUL.**
For authors who have ventured into selling physical copies through their website, BookVault and Lulu are the two most common companies for managing the task. Both are print-on-demand printers/distributors and do a solid job in terms of quality and reliability. On average, BookVault charges around half what Lulu does for printing, but Lulu works with Wix sites, which BookVault does not, and has the advantage of being a long-recognized player in the book-printing space.

Both options will also connect with either Shopify or WooCommerce, allowing orders placed on your site to be sent to the printer automatically, who will print and ship the book to your customer without you having to lift a finger.

9 PICK A STRONG SALES PLATFORM.

Because most authors will want to use BookVault or Lulu for the automated ordering and delivery, that narrows the field. BookVault integrates with Shopify, WooCommerce, and Payhip, while Lulu integrates with Shopify, WooCommerce, and Wix. That makes those four platforms optimal for most authors, but any of them can work.

That said, some authors don't need or want the automated delivery. Someone selling signed copies from their Fourthwall site can choose whichever printer they want, for example, since they have to order the books to them first, then ship them to readers. This is more work, but some authors prefer the closer connection to fans this can build.

---

10 LEARN WHAT'S NEEDED FOR TAXES.

Crowdfunding, subscriptions, and website book sales all count as forms of direct selling, and as such, you as the author-publisher will generally be required to charge sales tax/VAT. There are different requirements for different nations, but in many cases, there's a threshold below which it's not an issue. As soon as you pass that threshold, you'll need to collect and remit sales tax/VAT. For a state-by-state list of thresholds for sales tax nexus, see this site: https://www.salestaxinstitute.com/resources/economic-nexus-state-guide. This can be complicated, but don't let it scare you off!

Pro Tip: Don't try to do everything at once! Take your time, and ease into each step as you're comfortable. Although there's a ton of FOMO (fear of missing out) around this sort of thing, these tools will still be around once you get to them, and mastering one, then moving on to others, is probably a wiser play for most of us than trying to juggle too many new sales methods at the same time.

Don't stress this stuff. Remember that these are new sales channels we can explore and new ways to connect with readers, but at the end of the day, it's the stories and those connections that matter most. Take these things at your own pace, and enjoy the process of building new relationships with your readers. ■

Kevin McLaughlin

Kevin McLaughlin

Kevin McLaughlin is the USA Today bestselling author of 83 books. He writes mostly science fiction and fantasy, and is also the author of The Coffee Break Novelist and You Must Write. He's enjoyed reading and writing serials for decades.

Indie Author Gift Guide

The holiday shopping season is just around the corner, and whether you're shopping for the caffeine-fueled novelist who hasn't seen sunlight in weeks or the writer in the middle of their worst block, we've got you covered with the author's ideal gift guide for 2024. Prepare to discover gifts that will make any indie author's heart sing louder than their internal editor screams. From noise-canceling headphones to mugs smart enough to keep your tea hot, we've curated a list that's more useful than a thesaurus and more exciting than finding a typo in a rival's bestseller.

(Note: The following items have been verified by IAM staff members or received more than one hundred reviews and more than four stars on Amazon.)

THE AUTHOR'S PLANNER BY AUDREY HUGHEY

https://thewriteservices.com

Prepare to revolutionize your author's writing life with a smorgasbord of planners designed to transform a schedule into a well-oiled word factory.

Audrey Hughey's planner series can help your favorite author launch their new book without stumbling, focus their scattered thoughts, or track their journey from a caffeine-fueled dreamer to a slightly more caffeinated author. Whether you're a pantser or a planner when it comes to your books, Hughey has a productivity planner for every writerly personality, including 2025 author planners, undated planners, the essential book launch planner, and *An Author's Legacy*, a planner co-authored by Hughey and 20BooksTo50K® co-founder Craig Martelle to help authors protect their estate after death.

LIGHTING

Moon Light
$39.99
https://amzn.to/3gNM65d

Long days spent indoors during winter months can affect even the cheeriest writers. This globe sits compactly on your desk and mimics the light of a bright sunny day.

LED Desk Lamp for Dual Monitors
$55.89
https://amzn.to/3MxJbKF

This LED desk lamp is evenly illuminated, with no glare, no flicker, and no blue light hazard. Soft

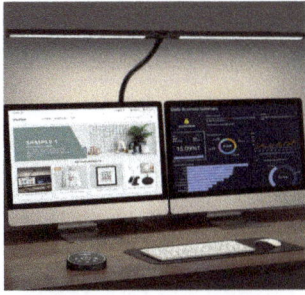

and even lighting helps to relieve eye fatigue caused by long-time use of computer screens. This light option is especially suitable for large workstations with wide curved monitors.

Govee Smart Light Bar
$59.99
https://amzn.to/3B1bDBY

Let Smart LED lights with twelve scene and music modes, a Bluetooth color light bar, and mood lighting create the atmosphere you need to write that perfect scene. With several dynamic aesthetic modes to choose from, you can experiment with the setting that fits your environment—or your character's mood—best.

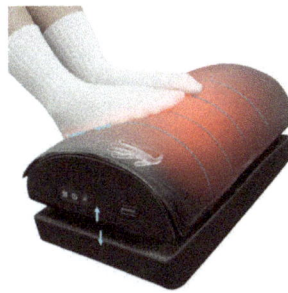

DESK ACCESSORIES

Desk Clamp Power Strip
$32.49
https://amzn.to/47rwo5V

For any author working on their own devices or looking to protect their works-in-progress, a surge protector is a must for your writing space. This desktop-mounted surge protector offers a 40-watt charging station with four PD 20-watt USB-C ports, two USB-A ports, five widely spaced outlets, and a six-foot flat plug to protect your devices from overcharging and overloading. The strip has an energy rating of 1,200 Joules and is made of fireproof plastic material.

Monitor Memo Board
$8.99
https://amzn.to/3MNshHL

This transparent memo board for your computer turns your monitor into the perfect storage space for your most-needed tools. Now your phone, notes, and character sheets can stay within reach during your writing session. The board can be moved to the right or left of your screen, and the phone holder is at the bottom, allowing you to charge your phone while working and keep the screen visible.

Heated Snailax Footrest
$49.99
https://amzn.to/3XoiTiH

The Snailax vibration foot warmer comes with three levels of adjustable heating that can be controlled with the touch of a button, providing fast warmth and improving blood circulation for your feet in winter. It's a perfect gift to keep your favorite writer cozy while they're stuck in one spot until they finish their latest novel.

COMFORT AND HEALTH

Under-Desk Treadmill
$287
https://amzn.to/3NcGX2F

Standing while writing isn't as difficult as it sounds, and walking while writing offers authors an easy chance to stretch their legs and work more movement into their daily writing routine. This treadmill offers two ways to get more steps: use the built-in writing desk, or drop the handrails flat and use it under a standing desk you already own.

Noise-Canceling Headphones
$299
https://amzn.to/3XwzpPc

Sometimes writers need to tune out their environment in order to concentrate. These Bose QuietComfort 35 II wireless Bluetooth headphones are noise-canceling and have built-in Alexa Voice Control—plus, they come in a limited-edition rose gold. Three levels of noise cancellation allow you to adjust your settings for a listening experience that suits your environment.

WRITING CHAIRS

Furnimart Swivel Criss-Cross-Legged Chair
$99
https://amzn.to/3ZmwSlt

If you're the kind to get antsy at your desk or need to shift positions often at your desk in order to endure longer productivity sessions, this armless office chair offers a sleek, ergonomic design with space to cross your legs or tuck them beneath you while you work. The chair offers plenty of durability and support for long-term use.

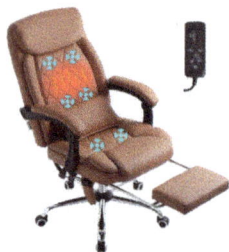

Executive Reclining Massage Chair with Heat and Footrest
$199.88
https://amzn.to/4enFJy9

With six different vibration settings available, this office recliner might help you feel less exhausted while pounding out your next manuscript. A comfy heated office chair helps your blood circulate and provides you with a regulated temperature during the winter months. This version can warm up to 100°F.

Futon Convertible Chair
$229.99
https://amzn.to/4d0HyzN

Not every author prefers to write at a desk. If you'd rather work from a couch or your bed, or just want to take a reading break in the evenings, this three-in-one pull-out sleeper and reading chair has two USB ports to charge your phone or other devices. The chair also has cup holders in the armrest and two side pockets for storage, plus extra storage space under the footrest.

KEYBOARDS

Typewriter Keyboard
$199
https://amzn.to/4dSxJoW

Setting the right mood in your writing space can be just as important as it is on the page, and for Historical Fiction or Mystery authors—or anyone with nostalgia for "the good old days"—the QWERKY-TOYS typewriter-inspired mechanical keyboard and tablet stand offers a chance to tap into your inner Ernest Hemingway or Arthur Conan Doyle with a realistic typewriter feel. The return bar and scroll knobs are functional; the return bar is programmable but defaults to an "Enter" key, and the scroll knobs function as both a page scroll and volume control. The keyboard is metal and works with Mac, iOS, and Android devices, and the heavy-duty tablet stand can support up to 12.9-inch tablets.

Multi-Device Bluetooth Keyboard
$48.99
https://amzn.to/4d4ZitY

Bluetooth 5.1 technology in this multi-device keyboard provides a cordless connection to your work, with an operating distance of ten meters and the ability to connect to your computer, tablet, or phone. The full-size keyboard includes the numeric keypad design, which makes typing easier and more comfortable than other wireless keyboards.

iClever Foldable Keyboard
$53.99
https://amzn.to/4elvoTi

For those looking for an even more portable option, the iClever foldable keyboard and mouse pad folds into thirds when not in use to fit in your pocket. The included touchpad and stand rule out the need for other gadgets, so authors can carry their writing desk anywhere and write whenever the feeling comes over them.

TABLES

Wacom Cintiq Creative Pen and Touch Graphic Drawing Monitor
$1,399.95
https://amzn.to/4cXraQE

The Wacom drawing monitor is a favorite among digital artists for illustration and design work. Multi-touch gestures, on-screen controls, two pen side switches, and more offer one-touch shortcuts and tactile control that can bring your graphics, cover art, or interior illustrations up a notch. The etched glass screen reduces glare and reflections while you draw and are designed to mimic the feel of a pen on paper.

Amazon Fire HD Eight-Inch Tablet
$59.99
https://amzn.to/3zrd3VT

It's important authors stay in the know about entertainment, or even just have a way to unwind at the end of the day. With the Amazon Fire tablet, stream or download your favorite shows and movies from Prime Video, Netflix, Disney+, and HBO. Enjoy your favorite content from Facebook, Hulu, Instagram, TikTok, and more through Amazon's app store. And of course, download and read your favorite books—whether they're yours or another author's—through the Kindle app.

Samsung Galaxy Eleven-Inch Android Tablet
$167.72
https://amzn.to/4daZvfi

Bring your ability to write or design graphics with you when you travel with the bright, engaging eleven-inch screen on the Samsung Galaxy tablet. Not only for work, this tablet's powerful speakers and slim, durable design also keep your music, shows, and games portable for writing retreats or conference travel.

MUGS

Self-Heating Coffee Mug
$89.96
https://amzn.to/4ef2y7z

If you have a habit of letting your tea or coffee cool when in the midst of a productivity sprint, this temperature control smart mug is the answer. With a built-in lithium battery, your drink can maintain a temperature of 120°F for up to two hours after fully charging. Enjoy hot drinks during long meetings or while working without frequent recharging.

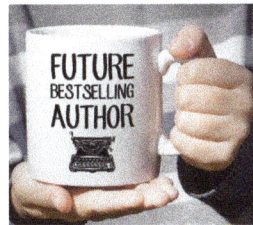

"Future Bestselling Author" Mug
$15.90
https://amzn.to/3XG8ssr

Every author needs a specialty mug with a mantra to motivate them toward The End, and this eleven-ounce ceramic "Future Bestselling Author" mug is a gift they will always remember and appreciate.

NOTE-TAKING

Rocketbook Core Reusable Spiral Notebook
$33.36
https://amzn.to/3ziGSrH

Every author has a stash of unused notebooks and journals in their closet, but Rocketbook's reusable spiral notebook rules out the need for more paper and provides a safe way to store your notes, story ideas, and outlines for whenever you need them again. Write on the page with the included pen, digitize your notes in the Cloud once you're done, erase the page with a damp cloth, then write again. Finally, a notebook with enough pages to house all those stray story ideas floating around in your head.

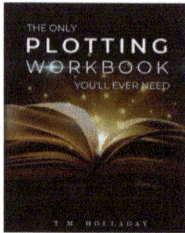

The Only Plotting Workbook You'll Ever Need

$11.99

https://amzn.to/3N2mTkx

Author T.M. Holladay knows there's more than one way to outline a story; his guide, *The Only Plotting Workbook You'll Ever Need*, offers a detailed walk-through of ten different methods so you can find the right one for your writing style. The workbook includes worksheets, timelines, calendars, and scene maps, with prompts enough to guide your story but not pigeonhole it if you want to try something new.

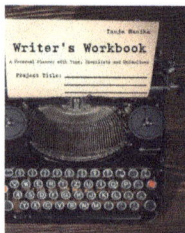

Writer's Workbook: With Tips, Checklists and Guidelines

$15.99

https://amzn.to/3XoWlhN

Even experienced authors can benefit from returning to the basics, and Tanja Hanika's *Writer's Workbook* is as much a guide to plotting as it is a guide to good craft itself. The book offers tips, checklists, and outlines for shaping everything from character development to story arcs while writing the story, but it also walks readers through creating plot synopses and other marketing materials for once the manuscript is complete.

CAREER ENHANCERS

Finally, *Indie Author Magazine* and Indie Author Training offer authors a chance to keep a finger on the pulse of the ever-changing publishing industry and to learn directly from thought leaders and experts in the field. Consider gifting subscriptions to the authors in your life—or to yourself—and keep on top of the latest resources, news, and trends in the indie author community, through monthly issues of *IAM* or webinars, courses, and discussions hosted on Indie Author Training.

Even if the author in your life has everything they need, you can still show them love this holiday season. A heartfelt message of encouragement, a cup of tea while on deadline, or a post about their books on social media—no matter the time of year, your support is one of the best gifts you can offer.

Know of any must-have gifts for 2024 we've missed? Let us know at suggestions@indieauthormagazine. com! We may feature them in future issues. ∎

Terry Wells-Brown

Terry Wells-Brown

Terry Wells-Brown lives in the lush California Zinfandel wine country with the love of her life; Don, and their two rescue pups; Jake and Buster. Terry is the author of the romantic suspense series Women of Wine Country, the contemporary fantasy series Earth Magic, and the international collaboration; Sisters of Sin. She is also the feature writer for Best Version Media community magazine; Woodbridge and West Lodi. Besides reading and writing, she devotes her time to her family, tribe, and her small community. During Halloween, Terry enjoys dancing as one of the Witches of Wine Country, and a couple of months later trades in the pointy hat for a red dress where she can be found impersonating Mrs. Claus.

LISTEN ON OUR APP OR YOUR FAVORITE PODCAST SERVICE

INDIE AUTHOR MAGAZINE

PODCAST

Hosted by Indie Annie

The Official

INDIE AUTHOR MAGAZINE

YOUTUBE CHANNEL

Behind the Scenes Author Interviews, How-To Tech Tutorials, and Tips for New Storytellers!

SUBSCRIBE

YOUTUBE.COM/@INDIEAUTHORMAGAZINE

Readercon 33 an Intimate Escape from Typical Sci-Fi Conventions

Readercon 33 this past July was a standout Science Fiction convention, but it looked different and felt more intimate than any other typical Sci-Fi convention I've attended. There were no flashy costumes, sprawling vendor halls, or multimedia displays vying for attention. Instead, I was surrounded by people deeply engaged in conversations about character development, world-building, and the art of writing itself. The hotel's meeting rooms were filled with discussions on themes and symbolism, and I was struck by how much more cerebral the experience was. Wandering into the dealer room, tables were stacked with books, and it was clear this was a place for those who love the written word.

For the four days attendees spent at the event, there was no distraction from media or pop culture—just the pure connection between authors and readers, united by a shared passion for storytelling.

Readercon is a New England regional literary conference that focuses on the Science Fiction, Fantasy, and Horror genres. Its thirty-third annual

event took place in Quincy, Massachusetts, July 11-14 earlier this year and attracted authors and poets of all levels in the Speculative genre.

While other Science Fiction conventions focus on fandom, media, and cosplay, Readercon features a near-total focus on the written word. The program hosts panel discussions, author readings, and solo talks or workshops. It also features kaffee-klatsches—intimate gatherings with an author—autograph sessions, and award presentations. Two major awards are also presented at the conference: the Cordwainer Smith Rediscovery Award, which honors under-read Science Fiction and Fantasy authors, and the Shirley Jackson Awards for Dark Fantasy and Psychological Suspense.

I had heard of Readercon for many years before I attended the conference virtually as a panelist. The panelists at Readercon are on par with bigger conventions such as Worldcon or World Fantasy Convention, and as a panelist moving up through the ranks, I didn't rate more than a single slot at first. As a poet laureate, I found myself invited to be a panelist and attended virtually again. But this year's event was the first time I decided to go in-person. I wanted to experience what made Readercon special to my fellow authors and learn why this conference came highly recommended by them.

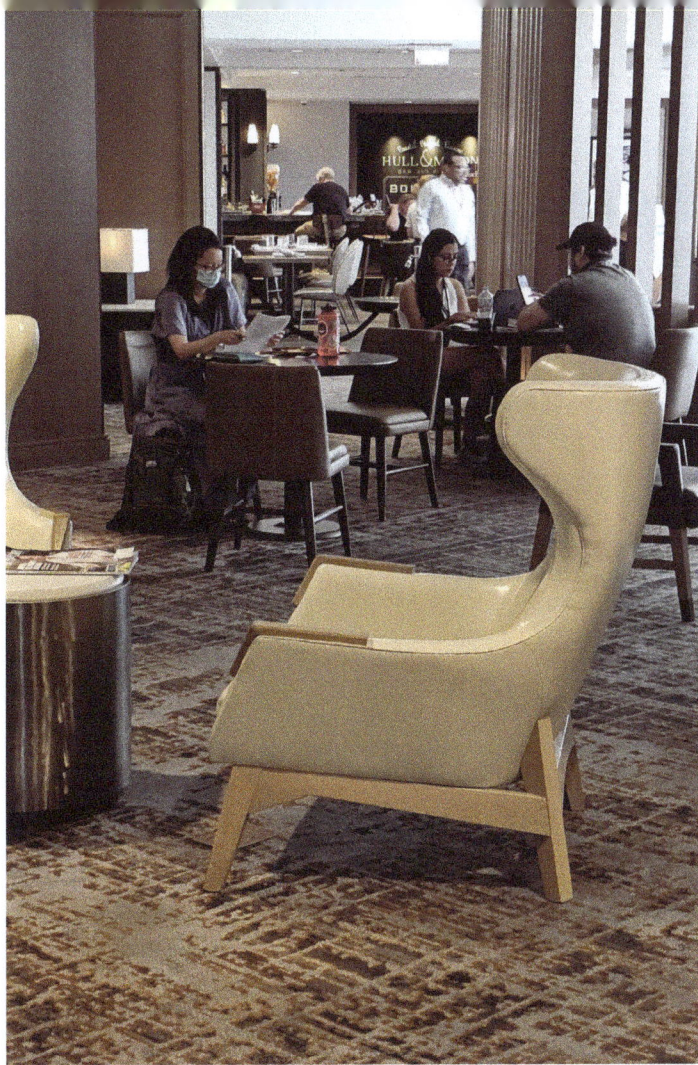

PANELS

Readercon spans four days and is packed with many panels, making it a dream for any book-focused writer or reader. The panels themselves cover a wide range of topics, but this year a lot of the conversations seemed to orbit around the ethics of AI—both the potential benefits for authors and the growing concerns about how it might affect creativity and publishing. There were also lively discussions on fanfiction, along with sessions offering general writing tips, from plot structure to dialogue. The vibe was cerebral and intimate, with a strong emphasis on the craft of writing.

The high quality of experienced panelists meant these were not panels for beginners. Everything was intermediate to advanced in level. Although I am an experienced panelist of many years, I certainly was kept on my toes and learned a great deal.

Most of the panels were designed with authors in mind, offering insights to appeal to anyone serious about the craft. There was a balanced mix of topics tailored to both indie and traditionally published authors, though you could feel a subtle elevation of traditional publishing in some discussions. While indie authors were certainly respected, the conversations often leaned into the prestige that comes with being traditionally published. Still, panels provided valuable information for both sides, whether you were interested in self-publishing or navigating the traditional path with agents and publishers.

GUESTS OF HONOR

This year's guests of honor were Amal El-Mohtar, a Hugo and Nebula Award winner and author of *This is How You Lose The Time War*, and Rebecca Roanhorse, also a Hugo and Nebula Award–winning author. Both authors were featured on panels, gave interviews, and hosted kaffeeklatsches at the conference.

DEALER ROOM

Even outside of the panels, the event was a literary lover's dream. Readercon's dealer room was more of a bookstore than a standard convention dealer room. Only books were for sale—no jewelry, crafting goods, or non-book-related items. The booksellers ranged from Larry Smith Booksellers and *Clarkesworld* to Bayside Books of Maryland. Small presses, such as Fantastic Books, Small Publishing in a Big Universe, Dragonwell Publishing, and more, had tables, along with smaller reader groups.

One table at the event was hosted by Broad Universe, a group of female Science Fiction and Fantasy authors who support women in the male-dominated genre. Every year at Readercon, they host a group reading, which they call a "rapid-fire reading." Each author reads for around five minutes. At the end of the reading, they raffle off books of the authors and give gifts of chocolate to the audience. Broad Universe is a nonprofit organization for new authors to make connections and gain a reading slot even if they are new to the field. They accept women and people who identify as women as members. You can find them at all major conventions, but Readercon is where they got their start, and they consider it their home.

There were also many authors selling books on their own. If they were in programming, they would either have a friend watch their table or close it briefly while they were away. Most of the authors I spoke to were positive about their book sales and were happy to be in the venue.

SOLO EVENTS

Finding ways for authors to connect with their readers was high on the agenda at Readercon. At the same time regular programming was going on, there were individual readings, kaffeeklatsches, and workshops. There were far more personal readings at the conference than I normally see at Science Fiction conventions, which was a real draw for Readercon. It is designed to allow an author more access to readers and the readers to the authors.

Kaffeeklatsches were held in a small room behind the bar of the hotel. Each session was an hour

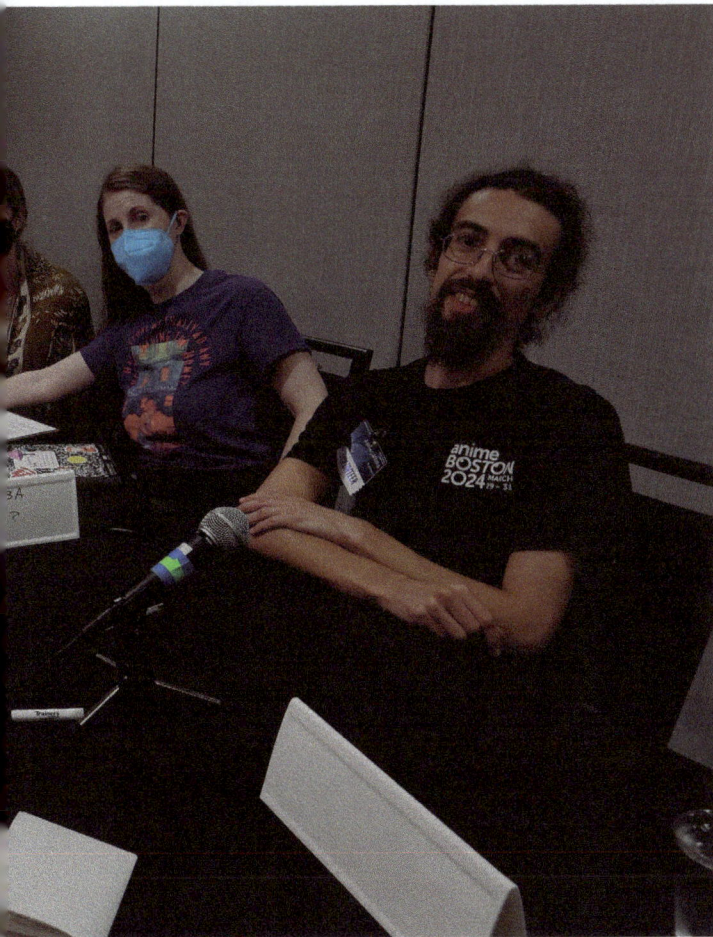

long, and there were always a pair of tables going at the same time. Readercon set up a free coffee service with cookies for all participants. Attendees signed up to join the author for a more personal meeting. The authors answered questions, talked about their future projects, and often performed a short reading

of their work if requested. Since it was for signups only, the location did not need to be in a high-traffic area of the conference. Kaffeeklatsches were more for authors with a following than for beginners. However, it was a wonderful way to gain readers' attention and create a memorable experience for those that met those standards.

Autograph sessions were held in the main hallway between the panel and reading rooms. A table was set up with a sign showing when each author would be available to sign books. It was a busy area of the conference, and people were always passing by, which made it easy for an author to sell and autograph their books during their time slot. They could also ask readers to purchase their book from a bookseller via consignment and then offer to autograph the books.

Workshops and meetups were in the same spaces as the panels. Workshops were casual classes, completed in an hour to ninety minutes and including a variety of literary topics, including writing poetry. One or two people led the meetups, but these were more for a group of people to express their interest in a hobby such as bookbinding. The meetups were interactive with the entire room, including the hosts.

The most common solo events were single author readings. I attended several of them during the conference in addition to my own. Every author had a sizable audience for their thirty-minute reading. The attendees relished the opportunity to hear authors reading their own work. Each author was asked intelligent questions by their audience and treated respectfully.

ADDITIONAL FEATURES

Readercon featured a con suite, where food and drink were offered for free to all attendees. They also stocked a green room with coffee and snacks for the panelists. Safety was top of mind; all partici-

pants were asked to wear a K95 mask in the conference area, and Corsi-Rosenthal boxes were added to rooms to aid the hotel's air filtration systems.

One night during this year's conference featured a "speed-dating for authors" event. Participants joined a table and took a ticket. At twenty-minute intervals, you moved to a new table and met another set of people. I found it to be quite the icebreaker, but my main chatting happened after the event, when I and a group of authors closed down the room late at night as we relaxed and talked about writing, life, and more.

CONCLUSION

Overall, this was an impactful experience for me as a writer and a poet. The quality of panels was great enough to interest me, even after years of speaking at conventions and feeling I had heard it all. I learned many new techniques to help me as a writer and made new connections in my genre, which will be an asset in the future.

If you are interested in attending next year's Readercon, tickets are available via the event website at https://readercon.org. The event will be held at a new hotel for 2025, Boston Marriott Burlington in Burlington, Massachusetts, July 17-20, 2025. However, it should still be a wonderful conference with plenty of literary vibe in the new location. ∎

Wendy Van Camp

Wendy Van Camp

Wendy Van Camp is the Poet Laureate for the City of Anaheim, California. Her work is influenced by cutting edge technology, astronomy, and daydreams. A graduate of the Ad Astra Speculative Fiction Workshop, Wendy is a nominated finalist for the Elgin Award, for the Pushcart Prize, and for a Dwarf Stars Award. Her poems, stories, and articles have appeared in: "Starlight Scifaiku Review", "The Junction", "Quantum Visions", and other literary journals. She is the poet and illustrator of "The Planets: a scifaiku poetry collection" and editor of the annual anthology "Eccentric Orbits: An Anthology of Science Fiction Poetry". Find her at https://wendyvancamp.com

Worldcon 2024 Immerses Attendees in Science, Scottish Culture, and a Celebration of Speculative Fiction

I've always dreamed of going to Scotland. I am half Scottish yet have never visited the country, even though I've longed to see Edinburgh and Glasgow for myself. Both cities are rich in the celebration of the arts. Not to mention, many world-renowned poets and writers are from the area.

This summer, I finally realized my dream at the 2024 Worldcon in Glasgow—and found a source of literary inspiration all its own.

"Worldcon for Our Futures," the eighty-second Worldcon, took place at the Scottish Event Campus (SEC) in Glasgow, Scotland, August 8-12. The Scottish Event Campus is in the city's heart, boasting an IMAX theater complex, an "Armadillo" structure for performances, a science center, and a planetarium, all of which were offering Science Fiction-related events during the convention.

Worldcon is an annual convention for members of the World Science Fiction Society (WSFS). The society is not only for writers but also for cosplay artists, painters, filmmakers, and more; the common theme is that your work is speculative. The convention is both an in-person event, with around four thousand-plus attendees, and online programming for people who would rather not travel. It is possible to attend Worldcon virtually and gain much insight as a writer if all you wish to see are panels, but if you want to network, attending in person is preferable.

PANELS

While Worldcon is not exclusively literature focused, its programming still heavily caters to authors, who make up at least half of the attendees. This broad focus means that in addition to literary panels, authors can explore other aspects of Speculative Fiction, allowing for a more well-rounded engagement with the genre. A distinct number of panels at this year's event focused on Scottish writers and their impact on the Science Fiction genre. Writing track panels were by writers speaking to writers, drilling in depth on ways to improve the craft.

Panels were not only about writing. Worldcon is more a convention for fans than strictly for writers. Television, film, podcasting, and many fandoms were also supported. I attended a geeky panel about the Disney character Ashoka, where five writers from both books and television featuring the character spoke in depth about her arc and where they hoped her story would go. It was great fun to listen to world-class screenwriters get their geek on and express their love for a character just as regular fans would.

I found that the panels were elevated in quality as compared with smaller conventions I've attended because of the experience of the panelists. Panelists were highly accomplished on the world level. Every panel I appeared on as a panelist was well attended, and the questions asked by the audience were thoughtful. My favorite panel was the Speculative Poetry Jam. Eight accomplished Speculative poets gave a reading to a full audience. The level of work by my fellow readers was amazing. I was honored to be included with them.

Most of the panels were recorded, both for virtual attendees and for in-person attendees to access later. Some panels were done virtually only via Zoom, which allowed additional panelists to participate who had not traveled to Scotland. I moderated one such panel for the writing track, for authors specializing in time travel novels, from my hotel room. There was plenty of interaction on the Zoom panel, with questions being fed from the Discord channel where the audience posted their comments as they watched the live stream.

GUESTS OF HONOR

Worldcon featured several guests of honor, who appeared throughout the convention in panels, interviews, and signings. Most were UK based. This is uncommon for Worldcon but not unexpected. The Guests of Honor included: artist Chris Baker—who works under the pseudonym "Fangorn"—fans Claire Brialey and Mark Plummer, author Ken MacLeod, author Nnedi Okorafor, and author Terri Windling.

There was also a list of special guests, who mainly appeared online for their panels and presentations: actor Samantha Béart, reserve astronaut Dr. Meganne Christian, editor Tanya DePass, Astronomer Royal for Scotland Catherine Heymans, author Tendai Huchu, and the hosts of CRIT Award–winning podcast *Three Black Halflings*.

DEALER ROOM AND ART SHOW

The highlight of any Science Fiction convention is the dealer room and art show. In Worldcon's case, both were side by side in one of the main halls. Because of the high ceilings and vast area, the tables of the dealers seemed a bit lost to me. Most of the tables offered books from publishers and small presses, but there were also scattered offerings of chain mail jewelry, stickers, and other craft-fair-level offerings. There was no true artist alley with tables of artists sketching and offering prints. Instead, most of the print art was in the Worldcon Art Show, a separate gallery at the convention.

The Worldcon Art Show was just as large as the dealer room, with both taking up significant space in a massive convention hall. The dealer room wrapped around the art show in a C shape, creating a seamless flow between the two areas. The art show contained an extensive selection of panels for the artists. Some artists did demos of their work, others gave tours of the art show, and a few spoke on designated panels devoted to Speculative-themed art. Most of the art on display was a step above what I've seen at typical convention art shows. The majority of the art was for purchase, but artists could set their pieces NFS (not for sale) if they were showing their work to attract the attention of authors or a small press needing book covers or other illustrations.

MEETUPS

Worldcon featured forty-five meetups for conference attendees to connect with one another outside of the scheduled panels. These were held in the back of one of the grand halls. The meetups included one for Star Trek fans, Doctor Who fans, and several for popular Science Fiction authors' fan groups, such as Octavia Butler, George R. R. Martin, Robin Hobb, and Terry Pratchett.

One meetup I attended was for fountain pen and stationery enthusiasts, the first of its kind at Worldcon. I brought a "penvelope" (a leather clutch purse designed to protect fountain pens) of some of my favorite pens and allowed others to try the specialty nibs my pens feature. Others brought ink samples to share or unusual papers. This meetup had so many people we overflowed the area. I also attended a smaller meetup for podcasters. There, we exchanged information about our shows and talked about production tips.

SCIENCE EXHIBITS

As a Sci-Fi convention, Worldcon didn't skip on the "science" portion of the genre. The event's science tract had plenty to interest attendees. Scotland has their own spaceport in the Shetland Islands, and alongside the other offerings in the main hall, members of their space program hosted tables to explain what they could offer Scotland and the UK. Many of their scientists gave presentations during the convention. There was even a fan meetup for female astronauts. Another fun exhibit was by a Glasgow museum, which showcased a virtual world accessed via immersive goggles. You could try on the goggles for free and enter their museum simulation. I asked to sit in a chair when I tried it out since other people seemed to lose their balance while wearing the goggles. It was all in good fun.

EVENING ENTERTAINMENT

Each year a Worldcon has been held in the UK, be it Dublin, London, or Glasgow, in-person attendees have had the chance to experience a unique performance or event as part of the evening entertainment. The first night of this year's convention featured a Science Fiction opera, *Morrow's Isle*. The libretto was written by guest of honor Ken MacLeod and inspired by *The Island of Doctor. Moreau*. The second night was a philharmonic concert featuring music from Star Trek, Star Wars, and Scottish symphony music about ghosts, goblins, and myths.

The following evenings were more traditional to the convention and had events that are a staple at Worldcons. Our third evening was the masquerade costume contest. Attendees signed up to show off their handmade costumes to an audience of thousands. Awards were offered for the most unique and best-presented costumes. On Sunday, the Hugo Awards were presented for the best in genre writing and in media. The Hugo is a much coveted award in the Speculative genre, and the competition is fierce. The fifth day of the convention ended early, so instead of formal entertainment, there were two parties hosted by the event organizers. One was a Scottish "Ceilidh" in the afternoon and the other a "Dead Dog Party," where people could relax and meet one last time with friends going all the way to 2 a.m.

CONCLUSION

I was astonished by how much Scottish culture was merged into Worldcon this year. I felt I was being given an education on the social aspects of the Scottish people and their achievements as much as I was learning about what was new in Science Fiction, Fantasy, and Horror as a writer and poet.

Beyond these cultural benefits, which were unique to Glasgow, Worldcon offers something less tangible but equally valuable: a sense of community. For authors, especially those who often work in isolation, connecting with fellow writers, readers, and industry professionals in such a vibrant environment can be deeply motivating. The discussions go

beyond surface-level chatter to delve into the craft and heart of Science Fiction. Whether you're attending panels, workshops, or casual meetups, Worldcon is a space where creative energy thrives and new ideas can take root. Attending isn't just about professional growth; it's about joining a conversation that shapes the future of the genre.

Next year's Worldcon will take place in Seattle, Washington, August 13-17. For those interested in attending, visit https://worldcon.org for more information on becoming a member of the WSFS. ∎

Wendy Van Camp

Wendy Van Camp

Wendy Van Camp is the Poet Laureate for the City of Anaheim, California. Her work is influenced by cutting edge technology, astronomy, and daydreams. A graduate of the Ad Astra Speculative Fiction Workshop, Wendy is a nominated finalist for the Elgin Award, for the Pushcart Prize, and for a Dwarf Stars Award. Her poems, stories, and articles have appeared in: "Starlight Scifaiku Review", "The Junction", "Quantum Visions", and other literary journals. She is the poet and illustrator of "The Planets: a scifaiku poetry collection" and editor of the annual anthology "Eccentric Orbits: An Anthology of Science Fiction Poetry". Find her at https://wendyvancamp.com

Trope Talks

THE FASCINATION WITH THE 'FINAL GIRL' IN HORROR

As writers, we often walk a fine line between tropes and clichés. Sure, tropes may echo other books in the genre or feel predictable as you read them—but as Jennifer Hilt, author of the Trope Thesaurus series, writes, "a skillful application of tropes sells stories." In her new multi-part guest series, Hilt explores standout tropes across a range of genres by breaking down a popular story into its many motifs. That trope isn't tired; use it correctly, and you can connect with readers by using these familiar themes—and your audience's expectations—to your advantage.

The Horror genre is the study of monsters, but most importantly, it explores our relationships with them. People often think of slasher films as the only type of Horror story, but the Horror genre is so much more. Recently, stories have tackled themes like war, politics, and powerlessness alongside more classic Horror tropes, leading to a renaissance in this genre. According to *The Guardian*, Horror novel sales are booming, with sales increasing 54 percent year on year.

The "final girl" trope is a Horror genre staple where a vulnerable female is the only one left to battle the monster; she is outmatched in size, strength, and preparation. It's a form of the "woman in peril" trope, which often involves the female requiring rescue. In the "final girl" trope, the protagonist saves herself by facing her greatest fear. It's a cathartic ride for the audience when a less powerful character slays a monster. It connects back to shared vulnerabilities in the human condition; everyone fears something.

As authors, our task is to decide:

1. How are my characters vulnerable?
2. How can I show that vulnerability in action?
3. How can that vulnerability resonate with the audience?

Want more "final girl" trope love? Check out *Hollywood Reporter*'s "Jodie Foster Has Heard the *Longlegs* Discourse—at the Gym." For a deep dive in this topic, also read Carol J. Clover's *Men, Women, and Chain Saws*.

To better understand this, we will examine the 2024 film *Longlegs*, where the final girl is a modern-day warrior recently assigned to the FBI serial killer squad. For other examples of final girl power, check out *Silence of the Lambs*, Grady Hendrix's *The Final Girl Support Group*, and Jordan Peele's *Nope*. Spoilers ahead!

In the 1980s, Lee Harper (**final girl, fish out of water**) joins the FBI serial killer task force. Her assignment (**quest**) is to discover why families have been dying inside their homes in murder-suicides with no forced entry (**forced proximity, violence**). Each victim's family has a daughter with a birthday on the thirteenth (**victims**). Harper and her boss's daughter share this trait (**ticking time bomb**). Harper is also an inconsistent psychic (**loner, scar**) who still shares a rural property with her mother (**forced proximity**).

As she investigates the case, Harper eventually realizes that the murders are connected to a cult (**found family, politics**). She discovers Longlegs's (**antagonist, hidden identity**) photo at her mother's home, awakening a memory of him visiting her (**scar, secret**). Longlegs, a doll-maker (**antagonist**), is arrested and commits suicide in front of Harper, revealing he has an accomplice (**the con, red herring, ticking time bomb**). Harper's mother (**antagonist, hidden identity**) murders Harper's fellow agent. Then, she shoots Harper's childhood doll, releasing a dark miasma. Harper collapses.

As Harper regains conscious-ness, Harper's mother describes becoming Longlegs's murderous accomplice **(blackmail)** to spare Harper **(final girl)**. Unsuspecting families opened their homes to Harper's mother, who delivered a possessed birthday doll **(MacGuffin)**. Once inside the house **(forced proximity)**, the doll infected the families with a murderous impulse **(ticking time bomb)**.

A dazed Harper meets her mother at her boss's daughter's birthday party **(victims)**. The doll has already infected her boss's family **(amnesia, violence)**. Harper **(warrior)** shoots her mother, fleeing the house with her boss's daughter **(victim, scar)**. The doll remains intact **(violence, ticking time bomb)**.

Tropes: amnesia, antagonist, blackmail, the con, final girl, fish out of water, forced proximity, found family, hidden identity, loner, MacGuffin, politics, quest, red herring, scar, secrets, suspects, ticking time bomb, victim, violence, warrior, woman in peril.

By the end of the movie, Harper is more than just a final girl; she's also a protector of her boss's daughter. She pleads with her mother to stop before she shoots her. In killing her mother, she destroys her family. Harper also damages the antagonist, but we're unsure if the monster is truly vanquished.

Wondering how valid female vulnerability is as a story vehicle? Check out this study by the Federal Bureau of Justice Statistics, "Female Murder Victims and Victim-Offender Relationship, 2021." Or better yet, ask any adult female how she feels about parking garages.

Harper is a final girl twice over, having escaped her childhood trauma only to revisit it as an FBI agent. Being a final girl means facing the frightening adult world. It requires losing childlike wonder and security because the character is thrust into survival mode.

As audience fans of the "final girl" trope, we're repressed trauma Doomsday preppers. Being a final girl is all about being prey, and Harper's journey allows us to feel that experience. It's cathartic for us because it's like a practice run; we leave the story thinking, "Yeah, I could've survived that."

Showing a character's scars and slowly revealing her secrets are two ways we experience this vulnerability. Harper's scars are numerous. She's facing a violent serial killer and battling her past. Revealing her secret psychic power makes her more isolated from her peers. It's an essential reminder to us as storytellers to demonstrate our characters' scars and secrets. That's where we find their vulnerabilities—and exploiting those vulnerabilities generates conflict.

Think of *Little Red Riding Hood as* the original final girl. Like Little Red, Harper struggles with things that aren't as they appear. She assumes her mother is a haven until that belief becomes a nightmare. Meanwhile, she's suppressed her major traumatic childhood event. Harper is an FBI agent and a psychic, yet her trauma-induced amnesia blinds her to the monsters she was living with. Although she's an adult, she is still a child emotionally, and her mother is the Big Bad Wolf.

Unmasking the monsters that Little Red and Harper experience saves them. They don't come out of the process unchanged; however, their trust in their loved ones shatters. They survive by becoming murderers.

This cathartic journey is central to all Thrillers, not just Horror. This theme is also present in Domestic Thrillers, where the protagonists must kill a once-loved family member who has become a monster. Facing life-or-death stakes brings out survival instincts, and the "final girl" trope proves that being vulnerable isn't a terminal diagnosis. The devastation afterward is a tale for another day, but survival against the overwhelming odds is the mantra of the trope. ◾

Jennifer Hilt

Jennifer Hilt

Jennifer Hilt is a USA Today Bestselling author of The Trope Thesaurus: An Author Resource, a five-book series. She has written twenty-four books across four pen names plus her urban fantasy trilogy: The Undead Detective. She works as a plotter and concept creator. As a frequent podcast guest, she has appeared on Joanna Penn's The Creative Penn, Bryan Cohen's Sell More Books, Matty Dalrymple's The Indy Author Podcast, and Kobo's Live Writing Life among many others. She teaches authors about story development in workshop and classes across the US. With degrees in linguistics and literature, Jennifer loves collecting dictionaries in unfamiliar languages, binges scandi-noir series, and shouts out tropes from the comfort of her couch. Visit www.jenniferhilt. com for her events, classes and workshops information.

May the Cash Flow Be with You

THE MONEY-MANAGING INSTRUMENTS TO MASTER FOR YOUR BUSINESS TO TAKE TO THE SKIES

The Force is strong in indie authors! Given a single worst-case scenario, we can probably spin up a story world in the throes of conflict. Unfortunately, that same imaginative bias can wreak more havoc on your business than a sandcrawler swarming with Jawa traders. Ambush can come from either side: a lack of financial data could make you assume the worst and quit too early, or it could lead to a poorly timed splurge on publishing tools you'll never use. Fortunately, there's more than one way out of a desert sandstorm. Use a few simple instruments to clear your mind, free up new creative energy, and decide whether those extra purchases—like those quality second-hand androids—are worth a second glance. Limitations always seem to make for better creativity, from a simple sonnet to George Lucas's *Star Wars*, and the financial limitations you create for yourself, a.k.a. a budget or a business plan, can shield your creative process better than a Jedi warrior.

Your publishing choices determine the kinds of income you receive and how your payments arrive. Adding more formats, merchandise, crowdfunding projects, or subscription plans makes for more complicated cash flow compared to earnings from e-books alone. But there are ways to simplify the process of dividing funds and keeping on top of business expenses. Using fixed percentages to calculate how much of each paycheck to save, invest in your business, or pay yourself—rather than fixed amounts—will let you break up large, irregular, or one-time payments while consistently building your business, and without cheating yourself or the tax office.

It isn't just about how much of your income to spend or save each month. Every indie author has a different business strategy and income stream, which means every money management plan should be unique. But whether your publishing payments fit more into the "delayed and detective," "micro, then mega," or "feast and famine" categories, there's an entire galaxy's worth of advice on matching your budget to your income situation, and we've compiled a few for you to explore.

YOUR X-WING'S DASHBOARD

To prevent crash landings, get familiar with your X-wing's dashboard—your money decision tools—before launch. Just like Luke Skywalker, you have a speedometer, a gas gauge, and an oil pressure gauge. "Your net income statement is like the speedometer … to let you know if profits are increasing or decreasing," Dawn Fotopulos writes in *Accounting for the Numberphobic: A Survival Guide for Small Business Owners*. Check it whenever you want to know if your marketing, pricing, products, and customers are working, and for ideas about how to earn more by working less. "Your gas gauge [is] the cash flow statement … [It] works like your personal checkbook" to keep your aircraft from running on empty. Check it to see which expenses to cut and if you might need a loan during a slow season. The "oil pressure gauge" is your balance sheet, or your net worth, and tells you what you have invested into your business and what it is giving you back. Authors can also note intangible assets such as copyrights, works-in-progress, or an established following. Check this whenever you are wondering if your cash and intangible assets are growing in value, if you need to write a few more books, or if you need to create more offers. The oil gauge measures the life force of your publishing business.

Pro Tip: If you've never formally tracked your business income and expenses before, a Google search should bring up plenty of free templates for Excel, Google Sheets, Notion, or another platform that you can customize for your needs. Fotopulos's *Accounting for the Numberphobic: A Survival Guide for Small Business Owners* also details how to set up your own budgeting documents.

Your dashboard can help you master your cash flow no matter your income pattern, but being aware of how and when payments arrive can help you make strategic and profitable decisions. Here are three common cash flow scenarios among modern indie authors—and the money management strategies they should keep in mind.

1. DELAYED AND DETECTIVE

Publishing royalties can arrive mysteriously slowly. Both authors who receive traditional publishing advances and indie publishers who distribute their books through distributors—IngramSpark, Baker & Taylor, Mackin, Follett, Draft2Digital, or PublishDrive—or directly through retailers—Kobo, Barnes & Noble, or Apple—will be familiar with payment confusion and delays. Even when everything goes right, authors who rely on these payments still often have to wait longer stretches between paydays. Kindle pays royalties once a month at the end of the month, approximately sixty to ninety days from when the book's sales were reported, and other retailers have different waiting periods and payment schedules. New releases can also create a "launch trough," wrote Joe Solari in his *IAM* guest series in March 2024, in which sales spike when a book initially is published, then die off quickly once the largest number of readers have purchased the title.

With an eye on your balance sheet, you can estimate your probable future income based on sales data, sales rankings, Nielsen scans, or royalty statements. Many distributors and short fiction or nonfiction markets withhold payment for thirty, sixty, or ninety days. Compare these expected sales numbers when the actual payments arise. Keeping track of current sales and withheld royalties may also help you find money that was never paid out and correct any administrative or banking problems. Your actual payouts may be lower than expected based on sales or "orders" data because of bank fees, foreign exchange fees, and/or reduction in royalties because of participation in a retailer promotion.

2. MICRO, THEN MEGA

Micropayments are becoming more and more common in the indie publishing world. Author-owned subscriptions of a work-in-progress and paid regular content on sites like Patreon, Medium, or Substack can help offset later publication costs of the completed project and provide a monthly payment that smooths out erratic publishing income. On the other hand, library checkouts or retailer subscriptions, which pay authors based on page reads or minutes read, can supplement income with small, unpredictable, and/or delayed payments. Macropayments are always welcome but are even more unpredictable. Rights licensing—foreign language, new format, tie-in merchandise, or serialization—or pre-publication of excerpts, or short fiction in the same story world, fall into this category.

As part of a larger publishing strategy, micropayments between mega payments can keep money flowing in your business during slow periods, increase your net income, and boost your balance statement, giving you more to invest in your business later on. Knowledge about your cash flow is a kind of superpower. For example, a running tab of your micropayments could be the inspiration you need to keep producing your subscription content. With the details at your fingertips, you can strategize to save up micropayments to pay for an opportunity such as a conference or book fair that might lead to a windfall payment. Or you might invest a percentage of your micro earnings into developing a line of book-related merchandise to sell in your online store.

3. FEAST AND FAMINE

Feast-and-famine payouts are common for authors who use crowd-funding projects to launch their books and to pay for their business expenses. If you're in the "feast" season of publishing, your balance sheet is your best friend to strengthen your business without exploiting the business owner—you. The temptation to pour all the money back into the business or to spend it all on an exciting vacation is real, but don't get too excited before you check your cash flow. Tally up your projected expenses until your next expected income boost, via your project's launch or your next crowdfunding event, and see whether you have already committed your resources. After you've divided up your winnings using your fixed percentages, consult your balance sheet to decide if it's time for an owner's equity draw, where you take money out of your business, or an increase in your salary percentage. Consider whether you want to reinvest some of the money into a professional membership, conference, contract, or software to make your business more valuable.

In times of famine, you may consider a new project. A when-will-this-break-even calculation can hone your focus and keep you from an avalanche of work that won't pay off … yet. Ruling out a project for now can free up your creativity, lower your stress, and de-clutter your desk. Joe Solari's *Author Capital Planner* may offer clarity about how long your newest idea will need in order to make a profit. The planner can also tell you whether your unexpected windfall has finally put you into position to launch a dream project.

Experience with your dashboard can tell you what you need to know and guide you toward creative decisions that are right for your talents and situation. "A business is a bucket for money," writes Michael W. Lucas in *Cash Flow for Creators*. "Money enters the bucket irregularly. Some months it gets a drop or two. Other months, money pours in." Keeping track of your cash flow can show you "how everything averages out" and what you need to make your publishing business fly. You'll be able to see your ideal publishing trajectory, because you're checking your net income statement, cash flow, and balance sheet, and you know exactly what you can do. In Michael W. Lucas's case, "Experience has shown me that four books in a year lets me at least scrape by."

Over time, your attention will pay off, and you'll come to understand the ebb and flow of your income enough to divide earnings confidently and adjust for fluctuations, or even to explore new business strategies that will move you into a different payment pattern. In the meantime, knowing your business's speedometer is working, your gas gauge is full, and your engine is running smooth and cool will free you to fly with confidence in the most treacherous publishing canyons. May the Force—and the cash flow—be with you! ◼

Laurel Decher

Laurel Decher

There might be no frigate like a book, but publishing can feel like a voyage on the H.M.S. Surprise. There's always a twist and there's never a moment to lose. Laurel's mission is to help you make the most of today's opportunities. She's a strategic problem-solver, tool collector, and co-inventor of the "you never know" theory of publishing. As an epidemiologist, she studied factors that help babies and toddlers thrive. Now she writes books for children ages nine to twelve about finding more magic in life. She's a member of the Society for Children's Book Writers and Illustrators (SCBWI), has various advanced degrees, and a tendency to smuggle vegetables into storylines.

Pigeonhole Publishing Finds New Audiences with Pocket-Sized Promotions

Marketing is a challenge that's hard to get right. You want to attract as many readers as you can, but you also want to attract only the right readers, who will love your book and want to share it with their friends. To boot, you need to get your book into reader spaces, places where readers regularly interact with one another and talk about books. Book clubs offer a seemingly easy solution, but how do you find the club that's right for your book?

Several platforms have attempted to provide an answer to the question, each in their own ways. Fable is a social app for readers that allows groups to set up serialized discussions, post about books, and leave reviews, but there is no author-facing element by which to track usage. Authors can only participate in book clubs if they create them themselves or have connections with the creators, though they can use Fable as a marketplace to sell the book to club members. NetGalley and other review generators promote books, but once they've delivered the book, most of the interaction stops.

Enter The Pigeonhole. The Pigeonhole is an

award-winning mobile book club that offers readers free interactive books and promises authors authentic reviews and reader interactions. Launched in the UK in 2014, the platform provides a modern twist on nineteenth-century serials. By releasing books in serialized increments, they encourage users to read together and participate in discussions. Bonus content, like playlists, author interviews, and historical context, appears in the margins to further spark reader engagement.

At this time, the platform seems to be one of a kind. It certainly defies the word's most restrictive definition. After five years in business, The Pigeonhole is the largest digital book club platform in the UK and has developed relationships with several UK traditional publishers. Now the company is looking to expand its reach to publishers worldwide, including indie authors.

READER EXPERIENCE

On The Pigeonhole, readers choose from a library of classics and new releases, sign up for a club or solo experience, and receive installments of a story, called staves, through the app on a prearranged schedule. Readers who join a club already in progress, or who struggle to keep up with the serialization schedule, will receive all pre-released staves at once and continue to have access to them for two weeks after the book club ends.

Available books are categorized as "In Play," for books that are currently part of a serialized event, or "At Your Leisure," for books that can be read at your own pace. Readers who select from the At Your Leisure list may create their own private book club with people they know, or read and react to the book on their own. Most of the books in the At Your Leisure section are public domain classics. All books include a free sample extract before readers commit to reading.

While reading, users can leave in-text comments and respond to the comments of other members of their club. Notifications can be customized or turned off, letting readers know when new staves have dropped or when other readers have commented. Readers can also access bonus material provided by the author through purple icons at the edge of paragraphs. At the end of the final stave, readers will find links to review the book on Amazon and Goodreads.

There are no fees required to participate in book clubs. However, for £2.99, readers get unlimited sign-ups, and for £7.99, readers get priority access to exclusive book offers and their name on the platform's patrons page.

HOW DOES IT WORK?

The reader experience may sound similar to Fable, Kindle Vella, or other serial reading services, but this platform serves a different purpose for its authors. While The Pigeonhole markets their platform to readers as "the book club in your pocket," their publisher-facing side highlights their review service as "the publishers' secret weapon." The Pigeonhole is not selling books directly; readers access their stories for free. Publishers instead come to the platform to build hype for new book launches and to generate reviews. Think of it as a curated selection of your most engaged ARC readers.

Authors release their books through the Pigeonhole app in "staves" that take about a half an hour to read. According to CEO Mark Blayney, this length was originally chosen to cater to commuters, but authors can set their preferred level of serialization or "let the whole book drop as a single stave so readers can binge-read if they want." Audiobooks may be incorporated into the serial, if you have the files available.

Pigeonhole staff use your marketing copy, cover imagery, blurb, and author bio to build a page for your book, which they then promote on social media and via the platform's email list. Authors are encouraged to share their posts with the page link as well. There is no minimum number of readers required to start a project. As for the maximum your club can hold, reader slots are released in blocks of one hundred to create a sense of exclusivity—the next block of one hundred will not be released until the first block is full.

Once readers have signed up to read your book, a dedicated project manager grants you access to the release, allowing you to engage and respond to readers' comments. These interactions between authors and readers drive initial efforts at review generation, but The Pigeonhole also contacts readers at the end of the serialization event to remind them to leave reviews.

Authors receive extensive data collections once the read-through is over. According to their authors' and publishers' guide, "Within a week of your serialisation's completion, we [Pigeonhole Publishing] will send you an Excel file of all comments." Additional information on how users read includes where they stopped, when they commented, and whether they left reviews. Fifty percent of Pigeonhole readers leave reviews, averaging fifty-two reviews per three-week project, according to the guide. An upcoming option to offer exclusive reading opportunities to Pigeonhole patrons, dedicated readers who pay for optimized use of the platform, may provide improved results.

GETTING STARTED

To promote a book through The Pigeonhole, authors start by choosing from four paid tiers. Once you've selected a promotional level, you complete an application that includes a sample of your book. The Pigeonhole may not accept your book if it doesn't meet the company's standards of quality and presentation. The platform may also reject a book if there are already too many books scheduled in a particular genre. If your book is declined, you will be refunded in full.

According to a genre interest chart Blayney shared, the most popular genres on The Pigeonhole are Mystery, Literary Fiction, and Historical Fiction, though other genres are well represented, including those in nonfiction and poetry categories.

The Pigeonhole highlights a few books from each list as "Pigeon Picks of the Week" to help draw attention to them. Authors who purchase one of the higher tiers of service may also have their book featured on the homepage or run additional rounds of promotion for the serialization event.

If you'd like to add your book to the At Your Leisure section as a perma-free option after serialization, you may do so at no cost. These books may be featured in book clubs set up for specialist reader groups, like those created for people in the care sector.

PRICING

The Pigeonhole offers both flat-rate and pay-per-review tiers, depending on your goals with the site:

- Flying Pigeon: a pay-by-results service reaching up to two hundred fifty readers (Cost: £17 per review generated, with a nonrefundable £100 deposit upfront)
- Nesting Pigeon: a tier offering the book exclusively to up to one hundred of The Pigeonhole's particularly dedicated patrons (Cost: £249)
- Homing Pigeon: a tier offering your book to up to two hundred fifty readers, both patrons and free members (Cost: £499)
- Racing Pigeon: includes the same features as Homing Pigeon, but with additional marketing and branding opportunities, data collection, and a videoed Q&A event (Cost: £649)

The digital author reading and Q&A event, which will be added to The Pigeonhole's YouTube channel, can be attached to the Flying Pigeon, Nesting Pigeon, and Homing Pigeon tiers for an additional fee of £150. Check for discounts on this, though. Blayney says the platform will have special offers while they build their list of author interview videos.

the pigeonhole

Whichever tier interests you, consider contacting General Manager Joanna McQueen before committing, as the website is not currently up-to-date.

POTENTIAL CHALLENGES

The company has undergone some changes in the past year, including new leadership, and is still working to improve the user experience for both readers and authors. In the meantime, McQueen responds efficiently to reported errors.

There is currently no integration with other author tools, and the app's security measures prevent direct email collection. So if you want your readers on The Pigeonhole to join your newsletter list, you will have to invite them to your own onboarding system. Previous free services for beta readers have been discontinued.

FINAL THOUGHTS

Authors looking to increase engagement and to build a bank of reviews for their work may benefit from The Pigeonhole's services. This platform's fusion of the reader community with author analytics could create a team of engaged readers who are more likely to follow through with reviews, and more importantly, invest in the author's future work. Despite the negative connotations of the verb, as a noun, a "pigeonhole" refers to a small cozy space, where pigeons or letters might rest. The Pigeonhole's online book clubs may offer your book exactly the space it needs to grow. ∎

Jenn Lessmann

Jenn Lessmann

Jenn Lessmann is the author of Unmagical: a Witchy Mystery and three stories on Kindle Vella. A former barista, stage manager, and high school English teacher with advanced degrees from impressive colleges, she continues to drink excessive amounts of caffeine, stay up later than is absolutely necessary, and read three or four books at a time. Jenn is currently studying witchcraft and the craft of writing, and giggling internally whenever they intersect. She writes snarky paranormal fantasy for new adults whenever her dog will allow it.

Indie Author Training Roundup

Since indie publishing got its start, authors have been seemingly at the whims of our biggest distributors—that is, until recently. As more authors explore outlets like direct sales platforms and alternative publishing platforms for their books, the options for greater royalties and better interactions with readers have been broadening. And this month, Indie Author Training is walking you through all of it.

If you've yet to discover us, Indie Author Training is a sister site to *Indie Author Magazine*, a place where indie authors can discover the ins and outs of the most popular tech tools on the market, the new publishing practices worth adopting, and how to make it all work with their business. From extensive courses with industry leaders to discussion groups with fellow students, you'll find information and support to help you in all of it and more.

In September, our series of webinars showcased how authors can build a direct sales path that lives on their website, with insights presented by *IAM* publisher Chelle Honiker. This information-rich webinar detailed how to set up a WooCommerce store to sell your books directly from your website and keep more of your royalties in your pocket. You can check out the replay here: https://indieauthortraining.com/webinars/is-woocommerce-right-for-you-unlock-the-power-of-direct-sales-for-your-books.

If you'd like to investigate this further, a course on the direct sales plugin, "Turn Your Website into a Sales Machine with WooCommerce," launches in October, also led by Honiker. Check out the details and register at https://indieauthortraining.com/courses-for-indie-authors.

We're finalizing the webinars for this coming month, so rush over to https://indieauthortraining.com/webinars to see what will help you in your career.

Have you discovered our tech tools yet? These product tours offer a quick whizz around a tool to show you its features and help you decide whether it would be useful for your indie author business. In September, we featured Sounded, an audiobooks site that allows you to produce and publish your audiobook in minutes at the price you choose. You can check out how at https://indieauthortraining.com/sounded.

If you're looking for training on a specific topic and we don't have it, drop into our suggestion group and let us know. You can also suggest product tours and webinars. Visit https://indieauthortraining.com/groups/indie-author-training-courses-what-do-you-want-to-see.

Finally, if you want to receive regular updates on the live events we're hosting or join in on the fun in discussion groups, create an account at Indie Author Training for free at https://indieauthortraining.com.

See you there! ◾

Karen Guyler

BUILD YOUR DIRECT SALES PATH

With Chelle Honiker

WATCH NOW

From the Stacks

An Author's Legacy

An Author's Legacy
Craig Martelle and Audrey Hughey
https://tinyurl.com/3a3sfuz8
One of the smartest financial decisions a creative can make isn't one that will affect anything during their lifetime. *An Author's Legacy: A Planner to Ensure An Author Lives On, Long After Death*, a newly released workbook by 20BooksTo50K® co-founder Craig Martelle and Author Transformation Alliance founder Audrey Hughey, prepares you—and your executor—for the smoothest possible transition of your estate after your death, including your intellectual property, works-in-progress, business accounts, digital and physical assets, and more. The book is not yet available, but anyone interested can fill out the form linked above to be included on the mailing list when the book is available to order, and those attending Author Nation can pick up a copy in person.

Google Keep
https://www.google.com/keep
A free tool in Google's suite of apps and products, Google Keep gives users a way to record ideas on the go and keep them accessible anywhere. Type out text notes and lists, add photos, or record audio memos; your messages are all stored on Google Drive and accessible across all devices with an internet connection. The option to color-code and filter your notes means you can jot down an idea without worry and return to it whenever inspiration strikes.

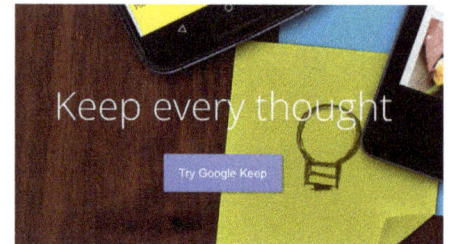
Keep every thought
Try Google Keep

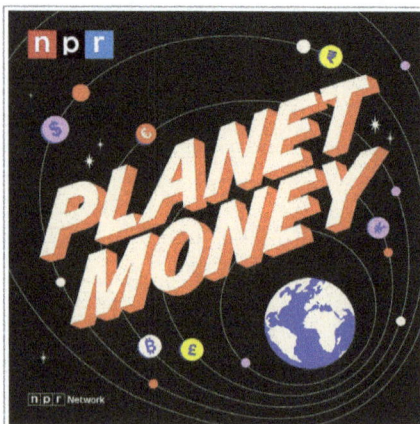

Planet Money
https://www.npr.org/podcasts/510289/planet-money
Planet Money's hosts know you likely don't have many burning questions about the economy, but they have the answers to all the questions you should be asking, in language you'll understand. Hosted by NPR, the podcast's twice-weekly episodes connect big topics and current events back to the economy, showing how the effects ripple outward. Whether you understand big-picture economics or just think you do, *Planet Money* will explain what you need to know—and make it more entertaining than that personal finance class you took in high school.

Putting Your Purpose on the Page

GUEST AUTHOR MEGAN HASKELL OFFERS HER ADVICE ON STRATEGIZING BETTER READER RELATIONSHIPS

Seasoned indie authors understand: for your business's long-term growth, quality often outranks quantity when it comes to reader relationships. But how do you ensure you're connecting with the right audience? In the second part of her series on finding your ideal author business strategy, Megan Haskell, co-founder of the Author Wheel, shares the importance of incorporating your story's message into your marketing. Find your story's purpose—be it entertainment, education, or inspiration, or a combination of the three—and you'll be one step closer to finding the people who like it best.

Have you ever thought about your purpose for writing? I don't mean the entrepreneurial business reasons but the impact you hope to have on the world. What do you want your reader to take away from your book?

Writing often begins with the ideas in our heads. We want to tell our story or share our experience. Too often, we forget to consider how our words will reach our readers on a head, heart, or gut level. However, dialing in on that reader experience can help shape our business decisions and clear the way for success. With your purpose in mind, it becomes easier to write your book, plan your launch, or create a long-term marketing campaign that will align with your readers' interests.

There are three primary purposes for writing anything for an audience: entertainment, education, or inspiration. Broadly speaking, fiction is entertaining, while how-to writing is educational, and a memoir might inspire the reader with a real-world story of overcoming adversity.

However, there are more subtle impacts that affect readers across genres, and your particular blend will appeal to a specific type of reader. For example, Andy Weir's Sci-Fi novel *The Martian* is balanced across the three impacts. It provides entertainment through life-and-death stakes, education in the character's science-based responses to his trials, and inspiration by encouraging readers to stay calm and problem-solve in the face of adversity. It appeals to a reader who wants realistic Science Fiction action with a message of hope and survival.

Other stories might have a stronger emphasis on one or two of the purposes. Elizabeth Gilbert's *Eat Pray Love* is inspirational and culturally educational, and Dan Brown's *The Da Vinci Code* is an Action Thriller that uses history and puzzles to its educational advantage.

Your purpose isn't a singular choice. More likely, it's a continuum, triangulated by the three priorities.

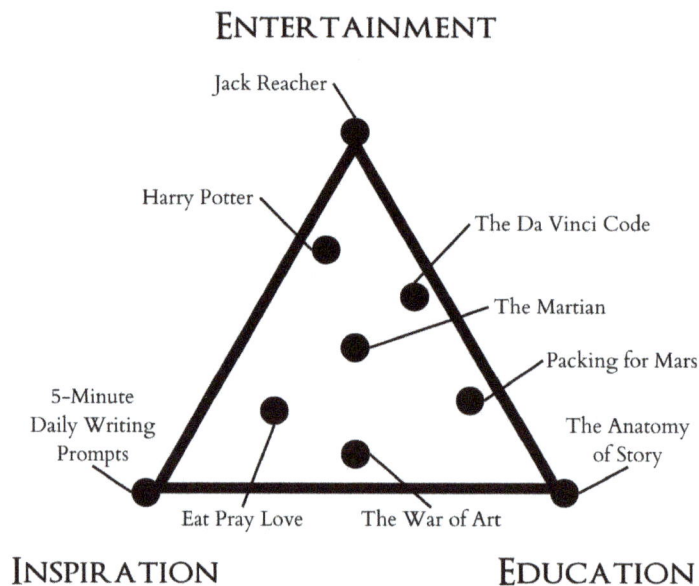

WHY SHOULD YOU CARE?

Readers will naturally gravitate toward stories—and to a sweet spot on the chart—that fits their own needs or interests. Understanding your writing purpose will equip you with the information you need to target that niche audience.

Let's say you write Historical Romance. If you, as a writer, enjoy historical research and include facts or true events of the era in which your book is set, then it's likely that your purpose is both entertainment and education: you want to tell a good Romance story while sharing your love of history. Your book might fall somewhere along the entertainment-education line.

If this is the case, tailoring your social media marketing to include historical facts, writing an afterword that explains where you've been historically accurate or taken creative license, or participating in an online fan group for that era might help you find and engage with your ideal readers.

By aligning your purpose with your reader's interests, you can find the sweet spot between art and commerce.

PUTTING IT INTO PRACTICE

Take a closer look at your own work. How can you use your purpose to reach readers in new ways? Here are some prompts to help.

For fiction, consider your setting, theme, characters, and tropes. For nonfiction, think about your voice, message, and subject. Which elements lend themselves to which impacts?

Prioritize the impacts for your book. Rank their importance on a scale of zero to three, with three being most important.

Plot each of your books on the impact triangle. Are they all the same? For brand consistency, they should probably be in the same general region. If not, you might consider whether a pen name would be helpful for marketing certain books or series.

Create a list of words and phrases that describe your desired impact on your audience.

Brainstorm new marketing ideas, taglines, or promotional opportunities you might use to appeal to your target audience.

Once you understand the underlying intention of your work, it becomes easier to communicate your message to the world and attract the right readers to your book. Suddenly, that elusive thing—your author strategy—goes from an abstract concept to a natural extension of who you are as a writer.

You've been putting your purpose on the page all along. Now lean in and share it. ■

Megan Haskell

Megan Haskell

Megan Haskell pens tales of myth, magic, and mayhem featuring strong female heroines and monsters of every size. She's the award-winning author of The Sanyare Chronicles fantasy adventure and The Rise of Lilith contemporary fantasy series, and co-founder of The Author Wheel Podcast and courses for writers. With more than fifteen years of writing and publishing experience, her goal is to help you Clarify, Simplify, and Implement your own best path to an author career. Find out more at www.MeganHaskell.com or www.AuthorWheel.com.

Taking the Mask off
Classic Horror Tropes

HOW THREE HORROR STORY STAPLES CAN APPEAR IN EVERY GENRE

When a writer approaches the Horror genre, deciding to leap into the deepest pits of despair and crawl out of it dragging a kicking and screaming manuscript, they often use popular movies and television shows as inspiration. They try to add jump scares and visual tropes to the written word. Unfortunately, this often falls flat, leaving them with the question, "What makes Horror fiction?"

According to the Horror Writers Association, Douglas Winter's 1982 anthology, *Prime Evil*, defines it as such: "Horror is not a genre, like the mystery or science fiction or the western. It is not a kind of fiction, meant to be confined to the ghetto of a special shelf in libraries or bookstores. Horror is an emotion."

So then, the genre can be surmised into an easy yet not-so-easy definition: Horror is whatever it takes to evoke that feeling—as the Merriam-Webster dictionary defines it, "a painful and intense fear, dread, or dismay."

What does this leave authors to work with? If jump scares and other Horror movie tropes don't land the same in fiction, what does?

The answer has been offered in countless Horror novels already, in motifs and themes that have appeared across generations of writers. Horror isn't unique in its availability of tropes to follow, and readers have already said what they love and expect, just like in other genres. But those tropes aren't exclusive to Horror, either. Well-known tropes from Horror novels are used, modified, and molded to fit other genres, from Thrillers to Romance.

Horror fiction tropes abound, but you don't have to write Horror to use them effectively. Read on to learn more about the tropes that any author can use to inject suspense, suspicion, and even fear into their stories.

"THE PLACE IS ABANDONED—LET'S EXPLORE!"

Often requiring some clever dissolution of disbelief by the author, the "we should go somewhere we shouldn't" trope is a staple for crafting stories that ooze dread. We know the characters will inevitably end up encountering something terrible that could have been left well enough alone. Stephen King's *Pet Sematary* is a classic example.

This idea of doing things that shouldn't be done isn't just popular for fiction's sake; it's in our human nature, and authors have made plenty of use of it in other genres as well. In the end, the author must break down the walls that would cause a character to turn away from the inherently bad place without a second thought. That sense of "Don't go there!" is the horror a reader wants to experience as they envision themselves in the story.

"WE SHOULD SPLIT UP—WE'LL COVER MORE GROUND."

Definitely cliché-worthy in Horror but in other genres as well, the idea that splitting up is a good idea tops the charts for dumb moves made by flawed characters. Seen from a mile away by the average reader, this trope must be cleverly handled to pull it off, but the result, if done properly, is a perfect amalgamation of two fears that make the story even more interesting: the fear of the unknown, and the fear of being alone.

When characters split up, the story increases in pace, the tensions mount, and the situation tends to worsen. The key here is to set it up early: give the characters a push, external or internal, so they can justify going off alone in their minds. Do this right, and the reader is along for the ride, knowing it's going straight to hell.

"WHO IS THE MONSTER AMONG US?"

M. Night Shyamalan is known for his popular movies and twist endings, so much so that even the twist endings are becoming a cliché. But his work in film proves that plot twists can throw a viewer—or in books, the reader—off what they thought was solid ground for a predictable ending.

Plot twists themselves appear in every genre, but with "the monster among us," the scary thing should be hidden in plain view for much of the story. Thriller and Mystery novels do this well, too, with readers knowing the culprit may lurk around any corner—even among those the protagonist trusts most—but Horror authors can use this trope to evoke a sense of intense paranoia or distrust in the characters. Not knowing who is who, or whether somebody can be trusted, isn't an unusual trope, but it is one that leaves a lot of room for creativity and ratchets the fear of the unknown up to the max.

As popular as it is, this trope may be so predictable that it could use a twist of its own. One suggestion is to humanize the monster, so that the good guys become the monster through their outward behavior. A classic example is *Frankenstein* by Mary Shelley, which saw the creature, Frankenstein's monster, subject to society's cruel rejection based on appearance.

— ❧ — ❧ —

Horror is a thriving genre with a rabid fan base looking for their next read, and while you can't put a jump scare in a book, you can focus on the emotions your stories evoke to keep your readers frantically turning the page. Inevitably, capturing a reader's attention is done simply by instilling unrelenting suspense and tension into your story—regardless of genre. ■

David Viergutz

David Viergutz

David Viergutz is a disabled Army Veteran, Law Enforcement Veteran, husband and proud father. He is an author of stories from every flavor of horror and dark fiction. One day, David's wife sat him down and gave him the confidence to start putting his imagination on paper. From then on out his creativity has no longer been stifled by self-doubt and he continues to write with a smile on his face in a dark, candle-lit room.

The Rhythm of Resilience

THE KEY TO REMAINING CREATIVELY FLEXIBLE IN A CHAOTIC WORLD

Births and deaths, sickness and weddings, holidays and emergencies—life keeps throwing curve balls, whether we are ready for them or not. Maybe your air conditioning goes out, and you can't write at home in a heat wave. Or an event creeps into your calendar a week before you'd planned, and you can't stick to your regular schedule. As professional writers and creators, we can't regularly brush off working during busy times. While we need to follow a regular work and writing schedule, we also need to flex around plot twists without letting them disrupt the flow of work entirely.

WHEN SCHEDULES SHIFT

If other responsibilities are rearing their heads and your work time has shortened or your schedule changed, here's your checklist to keep your writing—and other work—top of mind.

Prioritize: What are your bare-minimum goals? These are the things that absolutely must happen for your work. They also need to be realistic to the time you have; understand that, depending on the interruption, the day may not be "business as usual."

Plan: Break those goals down into smaller, manageable pieces. Create your plan, and make it as specific as you can to help you stay focused. Use strategies like time-blocking and lists to make the most of your work time.

Implement: Follow the plan. Be sure you include breaks and consider the new time constraints you have, but get to work.

WHEN WELLNESS COMES BEFORE WORDS

Of course, adjusting to life's interruptions is not always as simple as shifting when or how much you work. Some situations, such as

a death or illness, require a different response. For those times when you need more care and support, consider a broader strategy:

Focus on what you can control. What can you reasonably accomplish? What can you impact? These questions apply to both work and life and will help you establish what work you can do. Set the minimums you need to accomplish to keep your business going. In stressful times, life can feel out of control, but there are always things you can affect, and that's where your focus should be.

Take actionable steps toward your goals, no matter how small. Each step counts!

Keep going and build your momentum. Small wins can help you push forward, but don't go overboard and push yourself too hard.

Take care of yourself. It might look different from normal, but understanding what you need to do to care for yourself can help you manage. Maybe you need quiet to process, or time and space to grieve. Maybe you need a loud, raucous dinner with friends.

Emphasize progress over perfection. It will not be easy, and it will not be perfect. But every bit you add to your goals helps you get there.

We all want our work to go exactly as planned. But when something interrupts the flow, it just might change the work. Sometimes your experience will add new depth to what you've been writing. Sometimes you experience a boost as you get clarity on a situation. Sometimes there is nothing to do but extend your deadline and deal with the consequences.

And that's okay, too. Life isn't smooth sailing. We take those interruptions and build resilience that can help us in our future projects and lives in general.

Just keep going. ◼

Jen B. Green

Jen B. Green has lived in five countries on four continents with her three sons, two daughters, and one great guy. She reads anything that stays still long enough, plays piano, and bakes everything sweet.

After earning her Ph.D. in psychology, Jen tried writing a novel for Nanowrimo and was hooked! Her days are spent traveling the world, teaching undergraduate psychology, and wrangling her growing homemade army, but her nights are for writing Urban Fantasy with witches and werewolves.

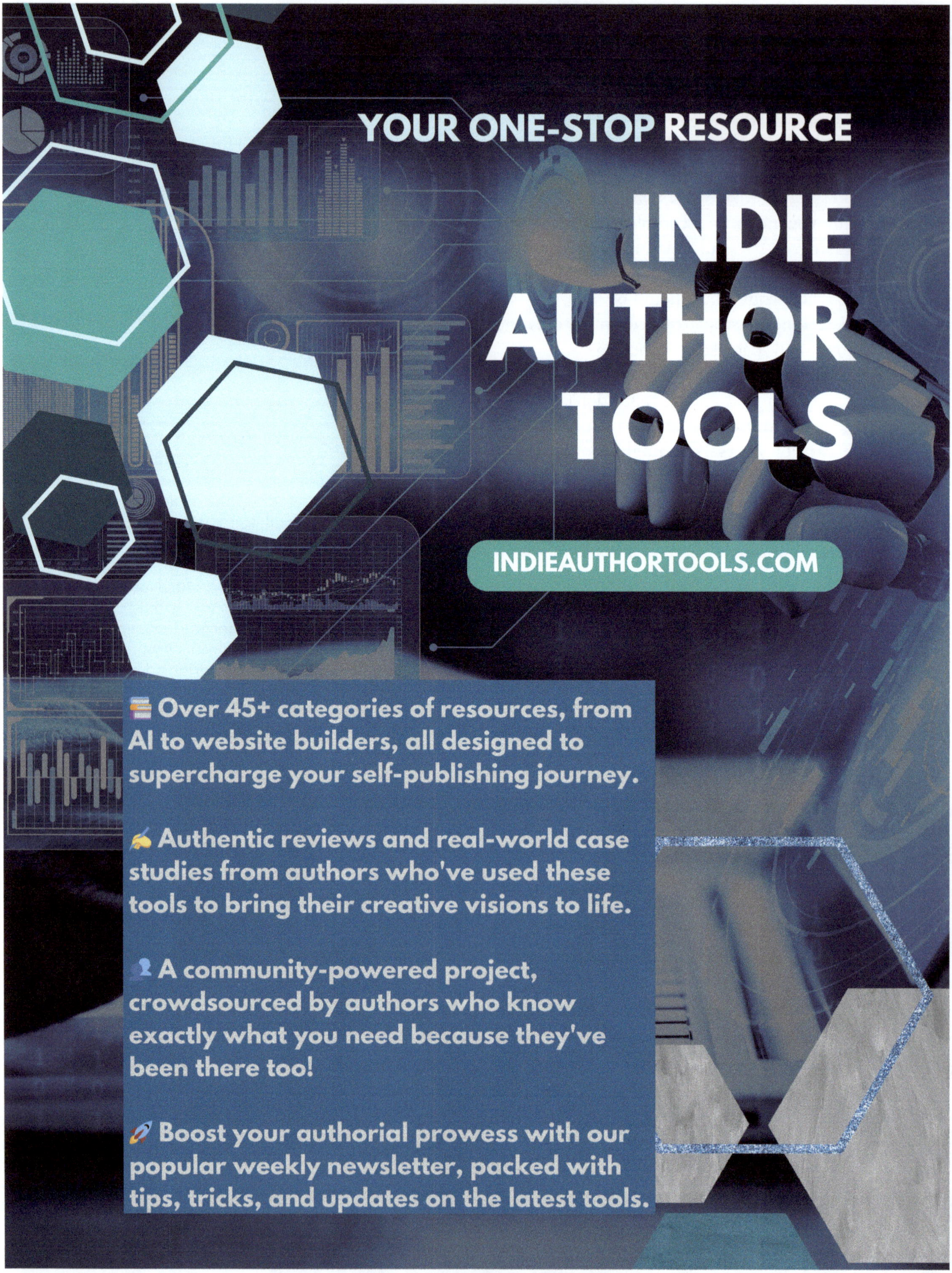

YOUR ONE-STOP RESOURCE

INDIE AUTHOR TOOLS

INDIEAUTHORTOOLS.COM

📚 Over 45+ categories of resources, from AI to website builders, all designed to supercharge your self-publishing journey.

✍️ Authentic reviews and real-world case studies from authors who've used these tools to bring their creative visions to life.

👤 A community-powered project, crowdsourced by authors who know exactly what you need because they've been there too!

🚀 Boost your authorial prowess with our popular weekly newsletter, packed with tips, tricks, and updates on the latest tools.

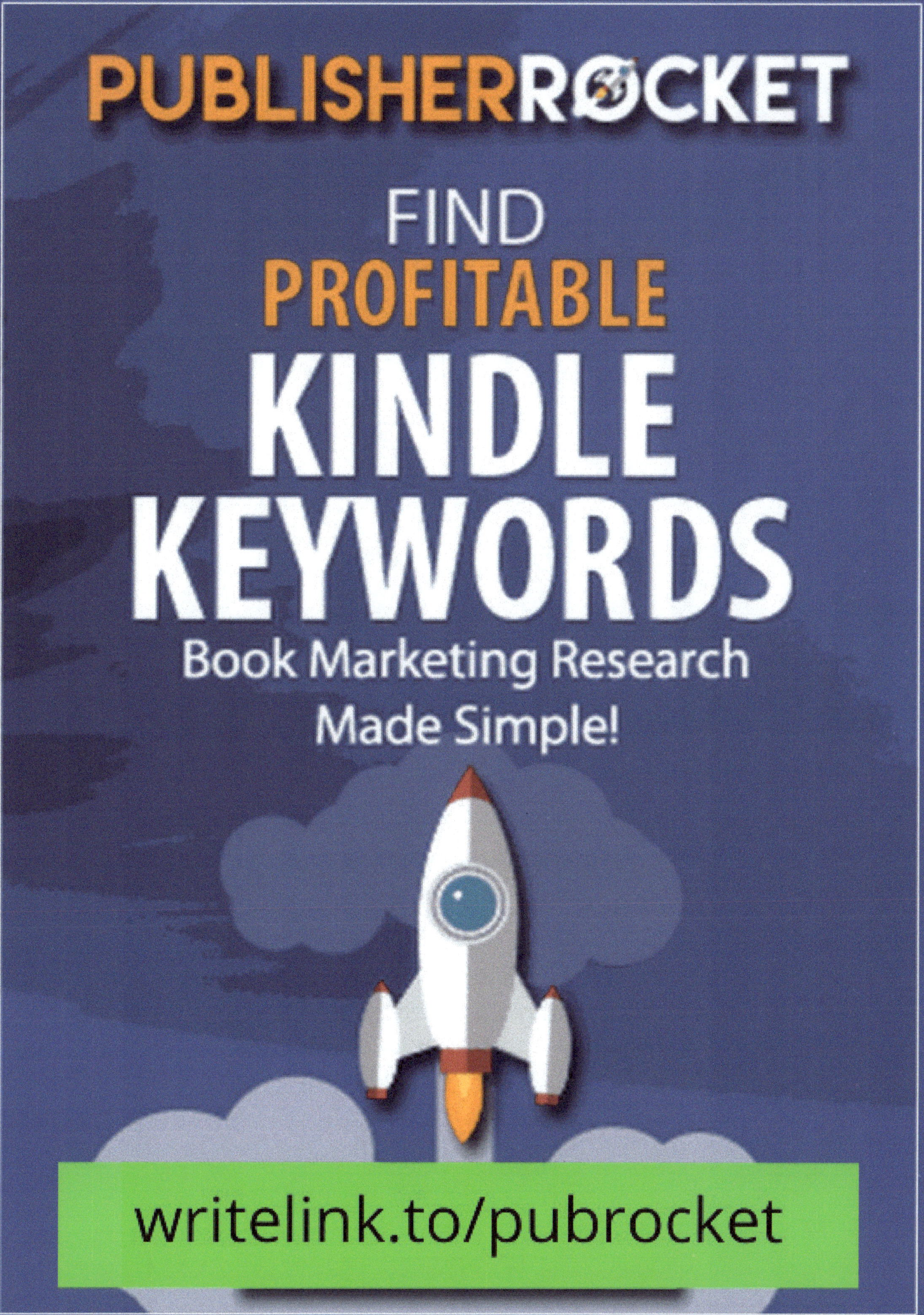
PUBLISHERROCKET
FIND
PROFITABLE
KINDLE
KEYWORDS
Book Marketing Research
Made Simple!
writelink.to/pubrocket

CLONE YOURSELF

Custom Chat GPT Bots

Harnessing AI's knowledge base and expand your skills and expertise in vital areas such as:

Life and Business Coaching
Mastering Marketing and Newsletter Strategies
Crafting Captivating Blurbs and Social Posts
Enhancing Time Management
Elevating Customer Service
Writing Compelling Ad, Product, and Landing Page Copy

And that's just the beginning.

INDIEAUTHORTRAINING.COM

www.ingramcontent.com/pod-product-compliance
Lightning Source LLC
Chambersburg PA
CBHW042341030426

42335CB00030B/3422

INDIE AUTHOR MAGAZINE

HELLO AND WELCOME!

I'm Indie Annie, and I'm thrilled you're reading this gorgeous full-color version of IAM. Did you know that you can also access all the information, education, and inspiration in our app? It's available on both the iOS App Store and Google Play. And for those that prefer to listen to me read articles, you can pop over to Spotify or our website.
Happy Reading! X

IndieAuthorMagazine.com

Download on the App Store

GET IT ON Google Play

Spotify

STORYTELLER
OPERATING SYSTEM

NOTION FOR AUTHORS

LEARN:

The PARA Method for Writers
Building Your Story Bible
Setting up Books and Series
Task Management for Writing
Task Management for Editing, ARCs, and Betas
Collaborating in Notion
Incorporating Other Apps into Notion
Automating Workflows
And More!

SIGN UP: INDIEAUTHORTRAINING.COM